CAN A SAVED PERSON BECOME UNSAVED?

Eternal Security vs. Works of Insecurity

Dennis D. Helton

CAN A SAVED PERSON BECOME UNSAVED?

ISBN: 978-1-7365344-6-5

All Scripture quotes are from the King James Bible

Address All Inquiries To:
THE OLD PATHS PUBLICATIONS, Inc.
142 Gold Flume Way
Cleveland, Georgia, U.S.A.

Web: www.theoldpathspublications.com
E-mail: TOP@theoldpathspublications.com

DEDICATION

I would like to dedicate this work to my wife, Christine, of 60 years.

Acknowledgments

This writer is grateful for his first pastor/teacher **Frank Sanders** and his faithful wife, **Jane Sanders** of *Agnew Road Baptist Church* (Greenville, SC). In the time of a harsh, hateful world, Pastor Sanders exuded a kind, gentle, and sweet spirit. He was also a zealous soul winner. Jane was greatly beloved by all of the ladies of the church and especially of the children. My wife and I will never forget them. We thank God for Frank and Jane Sanders!

PREFACE

FOLLOWING QUESTIONS ARE ANSWERED

- When Does **Everlasting Life** Begin?

- Does **Everlasting Life** Have An Ending?

- Can a **Saved Person** Ever Become Lost Again?

- Can A Person Be **Born Again** Multiple Times?

- **Salvation: Conditional Or Unconditional?**

- Are Believers **Blotted Out Of The Book Of Life**?

- What Is Taken Out Of **The Book Of Life?**

- Who Are Those That **Do Not Abide In Christ?**

- What Are The **Three Major Christian Denominations?**

- What Does The **Tares** And **Wheat Represent?**

- What Does The **Dog** And **Sow Represent**?

- What Is Meant By **Fallen From Grace?**

- What Is Meant By **Enduring To The End**?

- What Is Meant By **Working Out Your Own Salvation?**

- What Did Paul Mean By **Becoming A Castaway?**

- Who Are Those That **Draw Back Unto Perdition?**

- Who Is The **Righteous Man That Dies In His Sins?**

- What Is The Meaning Of **No More Sacrifice For Sins?**

- Inducement To Sin? **Eternal Security Or Arminianism?**

- Do Good Works Or Virtuous Deeds Assist Salvation**?**

- **Church Members Who Go Back Into Sin?**

- Can Anything **Separate A Believer** From The Love Of

- God?

- What Is The **Unpardonable Sin?**

TABLE OF CONTENTS

TABLE OF CONTENTS

INTRODUCTION

The majority of Christians can undoubtedly be divided into three major groups: Eternal life, Arminian, and Hyper-Calvinism. The writer will attempt to fairly narrate the distinctive beliefs of each. First, a brief introduction of them:

1. **Eternal Life (Free Will):** These Baptist Christians believe that salvation is a gift of God's mercy and abundant Grace. They believe that the saints of God are both saved and kept saved by the power of God (*I Peter 1:5; Psalms 121:5; John 10:27-30; Ephesians 1:13; 4:30; 2 Corinthians 1:22*). Eternal life brethren of the Baptist faith also believe that the Gospel invitation is open to all sinners upon their repentance and faith (*repentance is bound up in genuine faith - Luke 13:3; Acts 16:30, 31; Romans 10:9, 10, 13; Ephesians 2:8, 9*). Baptists believe that the saints of God are predestinated to be conformed to the image of Christ (*Romans 8:21, 23, 29*). Baptist brethren are persuaded of eternal life. They are usually referred to, by both their antagonists and apologists, as, "once saved, always saved."

2. **Arminian (Free Will):** These Christians believe, as Baptists, that salvation is free (*gift*) to all sinners, and also that the Gospel invitation is open to all sinners. However, they believe that they must maintain (*keep*) their own salvation or else become lost again and become a child of Hell. This theology of losing salvation is commonly referred to as, "Arminianism" (*losing salvation*). It is the most common belief held among Christians.

3. **Hyper-Calvinism (No Free Will):** These Christians correctly believe in God's grace for salvation; however, they teach that the Sovereignty of God voids man's free will to come to Christ for salvation. These

extreme Calvinists teach that God only died for a select few and not for the whole world. Hyper-Calvinists say that certain men are foreordained for Hell for no reason at all other than God's choice. They completely bypass the numerous repeated invitations for sinners to trust Christ, such as, "whosoever will, all, and the whole world.: The extreme Calvinists erroneously interpret the doctrines of divine election, predestination, and ordination. This theology is the least prevalent among Christians.

Hyper-Calvinists also incorrectly relegate all Christians to only two camps of theology, Arminian and Hyper-Calvinism. This ignores the third group of "Everlasting Life" theology (Baptist).

In this writing, extreme Calvinism will often be referred to as, "Hyper-Calvinism." Hyper-Calvinism theology is usually held by Presbyterian and churches of "so called" Reformed Theology.

4. **Christian in Name Only** There is a large fourth group of religious people who consider themselves Christian, but have not been saved. This fourth group encompass many different sects (it does not include pagan religions of Buddhism, Islam, Hinduism and many others that do not pretend to be Christian). This very large group of religious pretenders teach bold heresies. In spite of the false teachings of these sects, it does not rule out the fact that some may be saved. Some of these heretical sects of Christian imitators are even considered to be Christian by a few genuine Christians. All are within the sphere of **Christendom** (*area of professing Christianity*). These religious people may acknowledge the Christ of the Bible, but at the same time deny cardinal (main; primary) doctrines. A genuine Christian has experienced the spiritual, new birth called, born again (*John 3:3-7; I Peter 1:23; 2 Peter 1:4; 2 Corinthians 5:17*). These professing religionists are trusting their salvation to: good works outweighing their bad works;

catechisms; confessionals to priests (*called, sacerdotalism, sas'ar dot' l iz'am*); church ordinances (*baptism; Lord's Supper*). These unsaved people are victims of false dogmas and have been brainwashed sufficient enough to accept false teachings. Many cults deny the deity of Christ. Although many unsaved religious people are sincerely dedicated to their religion, they are sincerely wrong and have been deceived about salvation, not yet having genuinely exercised repentance and faith toward God (*Luke 13:3*).

There are many imitators of true salvation. Scriptures admonish all to turn away from false prophets, false teachers, and religious apostates of the last days:

> *2 Timothy 3:5:* **Having a form of godliness**, *but denying the power thereof: from such turn away.*

> *Matthew 7:15: Beware of* **false prophets**, *which come to you in sheep's clothing, but inwardly they are ravening wolves.*

> *Matthew 7:22-23: Many will say to Me in that day, Lord, Lord, have we not* **prophesied** *in Thy name? and in Thy name have* **cast out devils**? *and in Thy name* **done many wonderful works**? *And then will I profess unto them, I never knew you: depart from Me, ye that work iniquity.*

All that glitters is not gold. Just because a person is religious and even acknowledges the Christ of the Bible, does not necessarily mean that he is saved (*many false prophets deny a literal Hell (with fire) but believe in their version of a utopian Heaven*). The writer himself grew up believing the Bible (*even as he mentally believed about George Washington and Daniel Boone*), but he knew that he was not saved and certainly did not claim to be a Christian.

There are many unsaved people in the realm of Christendom who are vainly following unsaved leaders.

They love ritual (*ceremonial forms*), religious relics, and being accepted into a fellowship. Those that are trusting in anything other than Christ alone are mere professors, not genuine God-honoring Christians. There are **no** true Christians who do not believe that salvation is a gift of the Grace of God.

The new birth itself is **without works** (*Ephesians 2:8-9; Romans 4:4-6; 11:6; Galatians 2:16; Titus 3:5*). Salvation has always been and still is **a gift** of God (*Romans 6:23*). Good works are intended for those who are already saved, not to save them. All of our righteousnesses (*good works*) are as filthy rags (*Isaiah 64:6; Romans 3:10, 23*).

Beware of false prophets, false teachers, and religious unbelievers in the last days (*2 Timothy chapter 3; 2 Peter chapter 2; I John chapter 4; Matthew 7:15-20*)

Christendom Further Explained

Christendom is not made up of only genuine believers. Christendom is the part of the world or the sphere of the profession of Christ; it consists of both genuine believers (*symbolized by wheat*) and religious unbelievers (*symbolized by tares*). See Matthew 13:24-30. The tares (*imitators*) are those resembling believers (*wheat*). Again, many members of cult religions deny the deity of Christ. Apostate religion is identified in the Bible as the spirit of Antichrist (*I John 2:22-23; 4:15; 5:1, 5; 10-13; 2 John 1:7, 9-10*)

Christendom is a mixture of saved people and religious, lost-people in the field (*world*);

It is a mingling of saved Church members and unsaved Church members. Christendom includes the tares (*children of the wicked one*) as well as the good seed (*children of the kingdom*). The reapers (*angels of God*) will separate the good seed (*the righteous*) from the tares (*the unrighteous*) of the wicked one (*Satan*) at the harvest (*end of the world or age*). The tares (*noxious weeds; darnel closely resembling wheat*) are gathered and burned in the fire; so shall it be in the end of this world (*Mathew 13:36-43, 49-51*).

Many unsaved religious people are sincere but at the same time beguiled by seductive teachers that appear to be harmless on the surface. Large numbers of people are beguiled by **false prophets** who are expert at camouflage and clever concealment of bold heresies. Many of these false prophets are dressed up and paraded on television as apostles of Christ.

> *II Corinthians chapter 11:13-15:For such are false apostles, deceitful workers, transforming themselves into the apostles of Christ. And no marvel: for Satan himself is transformed into an angel of light. Therefore it is no great thing if **his***

13

ministers also be transformed as the ministers of righteousness; whose end shall be according to their works.

*I John 4:1, 6: Beloved, believe not every spirit, but try the spirits whether they are of God: because **many false prophets** are gone out into the world. We are of God: he that knoweth God heareth us; he that is not of God heareth not us. Hereby know we the Spirit of truth, and **the spirit of error**.*

Proverbs 14:12: there is a way which seemeth right unto a man, but the end thereof are the ways of death.

Unsaved Church Members

Unsaved religious people may lead outward moral lives and appear righteous unto men, even as did the Scribes and Pharisees (*Matthew 23:27-28*). Christ called the unsaved religious Jews whited sepulchers, meaning that they were merely cleansed outwardly (*white-washed on the outside*), but not cleansed on the inside. It is commendable to be outwardly immaculate and principled, but self-righteousness will not justify a sinner. Many unsaved church members, as well as secular members of society, live outward moral lives, but self-righteousness will be the doom of many sinners. Most church members, that are trusting in their own good works to get them to Heaven, do not even have good works.

Sadly, many unsaved religious people are only playing church by practicing rituals and honoring unbiblical dogmatism. They do not have the peace of God in their souls. These *unsaved* Church members will be greatly surprised moments after death. In the great day of judgment, the incurable, unsaved, religious people will make a final plea but to no avail:

14

Matthew 7:22-23: **Many** *will say to Me in that day, Lord, Lord, have we not* **prophesied** *in Thy name? and in Thy name have* **cast out devils**? *and in Thy name* **done many wonderful works**? *And* **then will I profess unto them, I never knew you**: *depart from Me, ye that work iniquity.*

Unsaved church members are foolishly depending upon:

> ➢ good works outweighing their bad works (*refuted in Scriptures*)

> ➢ church, temple, synagogue, or sect membership (*salvation is none of these*)

> ➢ sectarian beliefs (*not taught in the Bible*)

> ➢ cult membership (*opposes true Christianity; denies the deity of Christ*)

> ➢ sacramental salvation (*false dependence upon ordinances and rituals*)

> ➢ confession of sins to priests (*called "sacerdotalism"*). Priests cannot forgive sin. Sin can only be confessed to God, not to other sinful men. (*Believers are only to confess 'faults" to one another*).

> ➢ doing the best they can (*self-righteousness is hated by God*); man's best efforts falls short.

> ➢ keeping the law (*no one ever has perfectly and never will....except Christ*)

> ➢ treating their neighbors right (*many lost people do that)*

> ➢ paying all their dues (*impossible; Christ paid the full cost of salvation*)

15

> ➤ vain traditions of men (*secularism and humanism are total failures*)

*Ephesians 2:8-9: For by grace are ye **saved through faith**; and that not of yourselves: It is **the gift of God**: **Not of works** lest any man should boast.*

*Romans 11:6: And **if grace**, then is it **no more of works**; otherwise grace is no more grace. But if it be of works, then is it no more grace: otherwise work is no more work.*

Works for salvation cannot be mingled with God's grace.

(**NOTE:** Italicized words in the KJV Bible are not in the Greek or Hebrew texts but were supplied by the translators in order to give a clearer sense to the reader. Notice that the letters of the words 'is it" and "it be" of the above verse of Romans 11:6 are italicized [letter characters slanted upward to the right as to emphasize supplied words]).

*Romans 3:20, 28: Therefore by the deeds of the law there shall no flesh be justified in His sight: for by the law is the knowledge of sin. Therefore we conclude that a man is **justified by faith without the deeds of the law**.*

Also see Romans 4:4-6; 6:23; Galatians 2:16; Titus 3:5; Acts 16:30-31. Good works are specifically intended for those who are already saved, not to save them. All of our righteousnesses (*good works*) are as filthy rags in the sight of God (*Isaiah 64:6; Romans 3:10, 23*). Christians are washed from their sins in Christ's own blood (*Revelation 1:5; I John 1:7; Colossians 1:14*).

Baptist Christians

The first group of our three main camps of Christianity to be considered is that of the Baptists

(*Eternal Security*). These Christians are often referred to as, Once saved, always saved, people. The prominent belief of these believers is that **salvation is a gift** (*free*) of God, and they can **never become lost again**. God will never renege on his promise of eternal life, and it is non-negotiable. Baptists believe that salvation is freely offered to ALL men through repentance and faith (*repentance being inherent of genuine faith*). The writer will defend this position (*his own*) by listing some of the many Scriptures that support the doctrine of the believer's eternal life/*eternal security.*

Afterwards, the writer will critique, what he believes to be, the extreme positions held by our Hyper-Calvinist and Arminian brethren.

The words eternal and everlasting are used interchangeably (*same Greek word "aionios" of Strong's Concordance # 166*). However, there are times when the word eternal implies no beginning and without end (*as, God*) whereas the word everlasting may imply a beginning that is without end (*as, man*). Of course, both eternal life and everlasting life are used of the believer's security.

Everlasting/Eternal Life in the Old Testament:

Genesis 3:21; 15:1; 18:32; 19:22; **I Samuel** 2:9; **II Samuel** 7:14-16; 23:5; **Psalms** 26:1; 31:23; 32:2; 34:19, 22; 37:17, 18, 23, 24, 28, 31, 39; 30:3; 34:19, 22; 52:8; 55:22; 56:13; 62:2,6, 7; 65:3, 9; 66:9; 69:28; 89:29, 33; 93:14; 94:14, 22; 97:10; 98:14; 100:5; 103:10, 12; 116:6; 120:3, 5, 7; 121:3, 5, 7, 8; 125:1-2; 137:7; 139:10; 144:14; 145:14, 20; **Proverbs** 3:26; 10:3, 30; 11:30; 24:16; **Ecclesiastes** 3:14; **Isaiah** 43:25; 44:22; 51:6; **Lamentations** 3:31; **Ezekiel** 18:22; **Micah** 7:19.

Everlasting/Eternal Life in the New Testament:

John 3:16, 18, 36; 4:14; 5:24; 6:37-40; 10:27-29; 14:16; 17:11, 12; **Acts** 5:20; 13:34; **Romans** 4:6, 8; 8:1, 35-39; **I Corinthians** 1:8; 3:15; **II Corinthians** 1:10, 20, 22; **Ephesians** 1:13; 4:30; **Philippians** 1:6; 4:7; **Colossians** 2:13; **II Timothy** 1:12; 4:18; **Hebrews** 6:19; 7:25; 8:12, 10:14, 17, 39; 12:2; 13:20, 56; **I Peter** 1:4, 5, 9, 21, 23; **I John** 2:12, 17; 3:2, 9; **Jude** 1, 24.

This list of references is by no means complete. Many other Scriptures teach the security of the believer (*not the professing believer*).

Eternal life brethren are mostly Southern Baptists, Independent Baptists and others of like faith. These believers are convinced that salvation is wholly of God (*both the saving and the keeping*). Some Christians refer to the security of the saints as, Saving Grace and Sustaining Grace. Again, Baptists also agree with our Arminian brethren that salvation is offered to ALL people. Most importantly, Baptists believe, that by God's grace, sinners are saved freely (*Ephesians 2:8, 9; Romans 5:16, 17, 18; 6:23*), and by God's power believers are kept saved (*I Peter 1:5; Psalms 121:5; 2 Timothy 1:12; Philippians 1:6*). Again, Baptists believe that ALL sinners are invited (*free will*) to repent (*change their mind about sin, salvation and judgment to come*), and call upon God's mercy, believing on the Lord Jesus Christ for salvation (*John 3:16; Acts 16:30-31*).

Baptists champion the free will of men in the matter of coming to God for salvation. Both men and angels have a *free will*. How else could Lucifer have led astray a vast number of angels (*probably a third - Revelation 12:3, 4*), if they did not have a free will? God had no pleasure in creating mindless zombies and has chosen to give both angels and men free will in choosing

18

to obey, disobey, reject, or accept Him. Of course, God may, and has caused good men, bad men and devils to obey His will against their own when it pleased Him to accomplish a particular purpose (*as He did with Pharaoh, Balaam, King Saul, and Jehu*). However, this cannot be misconstrued to mean that God predetermines or consigns people to Heaven or Hell without their own will being the determinate factor.

THE HYPER-CALVINIST CHRISTIAN

The main purpose for this writing is to defend the unconditional covenant of salvation and security of the believer, from beginning to end. To this, extreme Calvinists claim to agree. However, some understanding of the Hyper-Calvinist's extreme view of predestination, election, and ordination is in order (*The extreme Calvinists do not like the label of "hyper" because it suggests that their belief is extreme and not normal*). The beliefs of Hyper-Calvinists and those of reformed sister churches are summed up in an acrostic called TULIP. Churches of extreme Calvinism (*not all are Presbyterian*) advertise themselves as reformed, meaning that they believe that they have a deeper theological understanding (*"reformed" means improved or corrected*).

The writer believes that Hyper-Calvinists are erroneous in all five points of their TULIP acrostic.

At the outset, the writer wants to make it clear to the reader that he believes that the **Bible definitely teaches Election, Predestination, and Ordination,** but it also refutes the extreme Calvinist position. Hyper-Calvinists deny men's capability to **repent** (*Luke 13:3*), and **believe** (*Acts 16:30, 31*) the gospel (*I Corinthians 15:1-4*). Of course, it was God who first came to the sinner polluted in his own blood. Though the sinner was totally polluted in sin, the Bible expressly teaches his free will to respond. It would be a difficult task to enumerate the many times that the Bible plainly teaches man's **human responsibility to choose**. The error of Hyper-Calvinism creeps in when men **emphasize an intellectual, twisted view** of election and predestination and at the same time ignore the often crystal clear invitations for sinners "to come to Jesus."

20

To the extreme Calvinists, the doctrine of God's election is opposed to man's free will. There is no conflict between the two doctrines. The problem lies in proud, stubborn men refusing to accept clearly taught doctrines.

The extreme Calvinists emphasize five points of their extreme Calvinism that is commonly referred to as the acronym T-U-L-I-P, an easy way to be remembered (*To quote another Christian author, "TULIP" is a "poisonous" flower*). Loraine Boettner lists the five points of TULIP in his book, The Reformed Doctrine of Predestination:

- ✓ **T** = **T**otal Depravity
- ✓ **U** = **U**nconditional Election
- ✓ **L** = **L**imited Atonement
- ✓ **I** = **I**rresistible Grace
- ✓ **P** = **P**erseverance of the Saints

A close examination of TULIP theology easily refutes all five erroneous points:

Total Depravity

Total Depravity (or Inability) – is the letter "T" of the acrostic TULIP, by which John Calvin meant that a sinner cannot come to Christ unless he is *overpowered* by God and given the ability to believe. "Total Depravity" is taught in Scriptures (*Jeremiah 17:9; Romans 7:18; Psalms 14:2, 3; 51:5; Romans 3:9-20*), but it is NOT man's inability to respond to salvation, as Calvinists teach. There is a distinct difference between "total depravity' and "total inability." The great problem is that man has a sin-cursed nature. It is not if you "can" come to Christ" but a matter of if you "will" come.

<u>Calvinists use John 6:44 to prove total inability:</u>

John 6:44: "No man can come to Me, except the Father which hath sent Me draw him..."

It is true that sinners cannot wickedly plead for God's mercy and grace at a time of their own choosing (*as in their final hours of life in hope of escaping the damnation of Hell; God cannot be used as a fire escape*). There is a deadline known only to God when His grace is no longer extended to the sinner. To most sinners, the death bed is his deadline. The Bible says, "Today is the day of salvation" (*2 Corinthians 6:2*); God's grace is now extended to ALL (*Acts 17:30*). Undoubtedly, all sinners of the past have had an opportunity to be saved.

*John 5:40: Ye **will not** come to Me, that ye might have life.*

It is not, "ye cannot" come to Me.

See John 12:32; 1:9; Romans 1:19, 20; 2:11-16; Matthew 23:37; Revelation 22:17.

*Acts 17:30: And the times of this ignorance (*the times before – v. 26) *God winked at; but now commandeth **all men** everywhere to **repent**.*

Could God or would God command people to do what they could not do. Here in Acts 17:30, the emphasis is that the Gospel is now open to the Gentiles, not just to the Jews. God had granted national repentance to the Jews, and now repentance is granted to Gentiles and Jews of all nations (*Acts 11:18; Matthew 28:19*).

The Bible expressly states in John 12:32 that Christ will draw **all men** unto Himself:

John 12:32: And I, if I be lifted up from the earth, **will draw all *men* unto Me**.

All men will be drawn unto Christ to some degree sufficient enough as necessary for salvation. Christ was

22

lifted up on the cross for ALL. Of course, Hyper-Calvinists claim that God only allows Christ to be lifted up to certain elected ones. They say that if **all** men are drawn to Christ, then **all** could be saved **if** he would be (*Note: "if he would be" expresses man's freedom of "choice"*). **All** men are drawn to Christ, but **not all** men will trust Christ as Saviour (*most will rely on false religion*). **God is no respecter of persons** (*Romans 2:11*) and God shall judge the secrets of men by Jesus Christ, according to the Gospel (*Romans 2:16*).

Total Inability

The extreme Calvinists invented the term "total depravity" (*or reprobation*) to describe their man-made philosophy of total inability. Total Inability could only be applied to a person who may harden their heart and darken their mind to the extent that God turns him over to a reprobate mind (*corrupt; depraved; damned*).

A sinner or blind pagan, seeking more light, will find enough (*as Cornelius in Acts 10*). Even before the Law of God was given, the heavens declared the glory of God (*Psalms 19:1*) and man was without excuse (*Romans 2:14, 15*). The gospel is in the stars. God will judge man, according to the light given to him. As the Spirit draws every man (*John 12:32*), and man has that true light (*John 1:9*), he is "without excuse" (*Romans 1:20*). Any man, once given that light, is capable of responding, and is held accountable if he does not.

Unconditional Election

By Unconditional Election, the letter "U" of the acrostic TULIP, Calvin meant that some are elected to Heaven and some are elected to Hell (*Institutes,* John Calvin, Book III, chapter 23 – "*...Not all men are created with similar destiny but eternal life is foreordained for some, and eternal damnation for others. Every man, therefore, being created for one or the other of these*

23

ends, we say, he is predestined either to life or to death.")

John Calvin said that the decision which determines the individual's eternal destiny is wholly and entirely God's decision, not in the slightest degree that of the sinner. Calvin's statement obviously and flagrantly disagrees with the repeated invitations in the Bible for sinners to come to Christ and be saved. Jesus charged the people of His day, "Ye **will not** come to me, that ye might have life" *(John 5:40)*. According to the false dogma of Hyper-Calvinism, it is not that these sinners "will not," but rather that they "could not."

If the brilliant Calvin had properly stated that all that die unsaved are foreordained to Hell and all that die in Christ are foreordained to Heaven, the writer would agree whole heartedly. Calvin does not expressly state this and merely substitutes the generic terms "for some," and "for others." The Unconditional Election of Calvinism is diametrically opposed to John 3:16. Election *(I Peter 1:2)* is conditional upon, "...repentance (*change*) toward God and faith toward our Lord Jesus Christ" *(Acts 20:21)*. God's Election looks back to His Foreknowledge and His Predestination looks forward to future destiny. We are elect, according to the foreknowledge of God *(I Peter 1:2; Romans 8:29)*. It is ludicrous for anyone to say that God predestinates some people to Hell and others to Heaven, without their own choice in the matter. That is an aberrant twisting of the Scriptures. To foreknow a person's salvation, as does God, does not militate against free will. Foreknowledge does not mean that God forces the person to be saved by a "so called" irresistible grace; neither does it teach that God denies a penitent sinner salvation.

Through technology, observations, and measurements of time, the astronomers can tell beforehand the date and time of a sun or moon eclipse, the appearing of Haley's Comet, or that of a red moon; however, this prediction does not cause the amazing facts to occur just because these facts are known in advance (*perhaps some think that they can cause them*). God can call the saved "the elect" because He knew in advance that they would be saved and NOT because He forced them to repent and believe. Besides, an **elect** body is a body of people that are **already saved**, not a group aspiring to be elected.

The elect are foreknown and the foreknown are predestinated to be conformed to the image of Christ (*not predestined to be saved*). Actually, any dogma of unconditional election makes God a respecter of persons (*for choosing some and rejecting others for no reason*). Calvinists say that God's selections are not based upon any action of the chosen. On this subject, Arno C. Gaebelein charged, "This kind of mumbo jumbo dogma, which **makes** atheists, is totally unscriptural and akin to blasphemy."

Predestination is all about the elect body being predestinated to be conformed to the image of God's Son (*I John 3:2; Romans 8:29-30*). The elect body speaks of those that are already saved. God has all knowledge (*omniscience*), and He knew who would respond (*free will*) to the Gospel message of salvation. If men possess no will to respond (*as mindless puppets*), an offer of the Gospel of Jesus Christ would be of no consequence and meaningless. Again, when the elect are spoken of, it is in reference to the future designation of a called-out people (*Greek "ekklesia"*) who are already saved and predestined to be conformed to the image of Christ (*Romans 8:29-30)*.

> *Hyper-Calvinists frequently misinterpret the Scriptures:*
> *Jude 4: For there are certain men crept in unawares, who were before of old **ordained** to this*

condemnation, ungodly men, turning the grace of our God into lasciviousness, and denying the only Lord God and our Lord Jesus Christ.

It was not that these men were pre-ordained to be ungodly, but being ungodly were ordained to this condemnation. These apostates of Jude 4 are the great enemies of the faith of Christ, turning the grace of God into lasciviousness (*wantonness; lust; lewdness*).

Even the Westminster Confession (Presbyterian Creed) advocates the fatalistic view of Hyper-Calvinism. It says, By the decree of God, for the manifestation of His glory, some men and angels are predestinated to everlasting life and others are foreordained to everlasting death.

If Calvin had specifically stated that devils and the unsaved dead are predestinated to everlasting death, and saved people and good angels were predestinated to everlasting life, this writer would agree. But Hyper-Calvinists say that God never intended to save some and foreordained them to be damned before they were born, and man cannot turn to God unless God forces them to. If some were condemned to Hell before they were ever born and had no opportunity to be saved after they were born, they would be blameless and the second death in the lake of fire could not be charged to their account. In the beginning, God knew those who would refuse to accept Jesus Christ as God's Sacrifice for sin; these are destined to the lake of fire, the second death of Revelation 20:11-15.

Limited Atonement

By Limited Atonement, the letter "L" of the acrostic TULIP, Calvin meant that Christ died only for the elect. Contrariwise, the atonement (*NT reconciliation*) is not limited:

26

➤ Isaiah 53:6: two **alls**

➤ I Timothy 2:4-6: a ransom **for all**

➤ I John 2:2: for the sins of the **whole world**

➤ I Timothy 4:10: Saviour **of all men**

➤ Hebrews 2:9: should taste death **for every man**

➤ Romans 8:32: delivered Jesus up **for us all**

➤ 2 Peter 3:9: **not willing that any should perish**

➤ John 3:16-17, 4:42; I John 4:14: the Saviour of **the world**

➤ Acts 10:43: **Whosoeve**r **believeth** in Him

➤ John 3:16: so loved **the world**...that **whosoever believeth**

➤ 2 Corinthians 5:14, 15: He died **for all**

➤ 2 Corinthians 5:19: reconciling **the world** unto Himself

➤ John 3:16: that **whosoever believeth**

➤ Revelation 22:17: **whosoever will**

➤ Luke 2:10: tidings of great joy was good **for all people**

Hyper-Calvinists claim that Christ did not die for all men and made no provision for them. If this were true, His blood was not shed for the billions of the "so called" non-elect, meaning that God did not love all enough for Christ to die for all.

John 1:29 says,

*"...Behold the Lamb of God, which taketh away **the sin** of **the world.**"*

Christ not only died for the sin of the world but for every man, individually, "for me." There is no such language in the Bible as limited atonement.

> *Hebrews 2:9: But we see Jesus, who was made a little lower than the angels for the suffering of death, crowned with glory and honour, that He by the grace of God should taste death* **for every man***.*

First Timothy 4:10 tells us of "the living God, who is **the Saviour of all men**, specially of those that believe." Obviously, God is potentially a Saviour to them who have not believed. Jesus is the propitiation for our sins: and not for ours only, but also for the sins of **the whole world** (*I John 2:2; 2 Peter 3:9*).

Jesus gave Himself a ransom **for all:**

> *I Timothy 2:4-6: Who will have* **all men** *to be saved, and to come unto the knowledge of the truth. For there is One God and* **One Mediator** *between God and men, the Man (God-man) Christ Jesus; Who gave Himself a ransom* **for all***, to be testified in due time.*

"All" is all inclusive and excludes no one.

Christ has made peace through the blood of His cross for **all** things whether they be things in earth or things in Heaven (*Colossians 1:20*).

> *For God sent not His son into* **the world** *to condemn the world; but that* **the world** *through Him might be saved (John 3:17).*

> *2 Peter 3:9: The Lord is not slack concerning His promise, as some men count slackness; but is longsuffering to us-ward, not willing that any should perish, but that* **all** *should come to repentance.*

> *2 Corinthians 5:14-15: For the love of Christ constraineth us, because we thus judge, that if* **One**

died for all, then were all dead: And that He died for all, that they which live should not henceforth live unto themselves, but unto Him which died for them, and rose again.

If Christ died for **all**, then no one is excluded. If Christ did not die for **all**, there would be a plain contradiction in Scriptures. Christ died **for all** *(II Corinthians 5:19)*.

The Gospel excludes none who do not exclude themselves. What part of the word, **all,** do our Hyper-Calvinist brethren not understand?

One writer aptly stated, Do not covet to be wise above what is written. When the

Scriptures say, whosoever will, let him come, and that **all** may come, who is to be wiser above that? Who is unwise enough to take away whosoever will out of the Bible?

*Romans 10:13: For **whosoever** shall call upon the name of the Lord shall be saved.*

There is no sinner that is beyond God's mercy and forgiveness (unless he continues on in the **unpardonable sin of unbelief**). In I Corinthians 6:9-11, we see a list of believers who formerly had been vile sinners (Viz., adulterers; fornicators; idolaters; effeminate; abusers of themselves with mankind; thieves; covetous; drunkards; revilers; extortioners; et al). If these vilest of sinners could come for salvation, certainly, the door is open to **all** other sinners. Even the Apostle Paul (former Saul) had beforehand imprisoned Christians, even to the consenting unto their death.

Christ died for all, but TULIP's limited atonement would require both the Bible and the dictionary to be rewritten. To Hyper-Calvinists, all does not mean all; the world does not mean the world; whosoever does not mean whosoever. They add to the Word and twist its true meaning.

Irresistible Grace

By Irresistible Grace, the letter "I" of the acrostic TULIP, Calvin meant that God forces (*overpowers*) the elect to be saved. They cannot resist this special irresistible grace limited to just them. But God does not compel a man to be saved that does not want to be saved (duh). Too, **the elect are already saved; it is their future destiny that is foreordained.**

The irresistible grace of Calvinism implies that those not elected to Heaven are irresistibly damned to Hell; however, only stubborn unbelievers, and rebellious Christ rejecters are predestinated and doomed to Hell.

Calvin taught that man has no part in salvation and cannot respond to the invitation to be saved. Of course, man has no part in the miraculous transformation of the new birth itself, but man does have the responsibility to respond in that he is free to believe the Gospel. Men also do **resist** (*free will*) the Spirit of God. Scriptures speak nowhere about irresistible grace, a "so-called" saving grace forced upon one who does not desire it.

The free will of man is explicitly stated in Acts 7:51, "Ye stiffnecked and uncircumcised in heart and ears, ye do always **resist** (*free will*) the Holy Ghost: as your fathers did, so do ye." (**Resist:** *oppose; fend off; stand against; will against*).

The grace of God is spoken of as a virtuous and loving attitude of God, not as an irresistible power forcing one to be saved. God does not force men to resist Him in the matter of salvation. The very reason that Christ came to earth was to seek and save the lost.

Jesus said in Luke 13:34,

*How often would I have gathered thy children together, as a hen doth gather her brood under her wings, and **ye would not** (it is not, could not).*

Jesus would have, but **they would not.** If a "so called" irresistible grace prevailed, they could not have resisted. This Scripture plainly says, **ye would not.** Although this passion is judicially expressed toward Israel, it also applies to individuals.

*Proverbs 1:24-26: Because I have called, and **ye refused**; I have stretched out My hand, and **no man regarded**; But ye have **set at nought all My counsel**, and **would none of My reproof**: I also will laugh at your calamity; I will mock when your fear cometh.*

Where is the irresistible grace here? God calls and man refuses (*resists*). Men do refuse God's call (*John 5:40; Acts 7:51; John 1:12*).

Scriptures clearly state that God is no respecter of persons (*Romans 2:11*); if that is true (*and it is*), then "so called" irresistible grace is merely a religious dogma and not a viable Bible doctrine. The basis for salvation is, What do you think about Jesus Christ, whose Son is He? Will you believe in Him? (*John 3:16, 18, 36; Acts 16:30-31*). This is what determines salvation, not a man-made indefensible dogmatism of an irresistible grace. It is he that believes (*John 3:16; Romans 10:13; Ephesians 2:8, 9; John 3:3-7*). Again, Hyper-Calvinists do not believe that man has either the freedom to believe or the freedom to resist.

Perseverance of the Saints

Perseverance of the Saints is the letter "P" of the acrostic TULIP. Whatever Calvin meant by perseverance of the Saints, it certainly does not depend upon the saint's personal perseverance and strength in order to continue in salvation. Saints do not persevere by their own works or faithfulness. Salvation is not **obtained** by good works, and neither is salvation **retained** by good works. **Preservation** of the saints would be a much better term if Calvinists would define eternal life as the Bible teaches (*Jude 1*). It is God who **preserves** the saints (*Jude 1:1, 24; 2 Timothy 1:12; I Peter 1:5; Psalms 121:5; Ephesians 4:40; Hebrews 13:5*). It is not the saints who persevere, but the blessed Holy Spirit. It is His holding out, not that of the saints. Philippians 1:6 expressly states, Being confident of this very thing, that He which hath begun a good work in you will perform it until the day of Jesus Christ. We are **kept** by the power of God (*I Peter 1:4-5*) and sealed unto the day of redemption (*Ephesians 1:13; 4:30; 2 Corinthians 1:22*).Saints do not overcome by persevering; the victory that overcometh the world is our faith in Christ, not our flesh (*I John 5:4-5*).

Hyper-Calvinists also love to justify their extreme view of election by saying that we were dead in our trespasses and sins (*Romans 5:12),* and being dead, could not move, walk, respond, nor do anything. They then go on to say that God elected some to respond. However, God is no respecter of persons (*Romans 2:11*). While it is true that all people were dead in trespasses and sin, and God came to us first when we were polluted in our own blood, it is not true that God closed the whosoever will invitation to sinners. If only **some** could respond, John 3:16 has no meaning. Bring home the missionaries, evangelists, and soul-winners! Evangelists are not sent out to preach only to a select body of sinners but to the **whole world** of lost sinners. Those that respond to the Gospel are foreknown by God, elected to salvation, and predestined to be conformed to the image of Christ (*Romans 8:29*).

Hyper-Calvinists also erroneously teach that since a sinner is dead in trespasses and sin, and cannot respond to anything, he must be born again in order to be saved and have life and be able to respond to the call of God. That may sound logical to the intellectual carnal mind,, but it is not according to Scriptures. These Calvinists suffer from the perennial "horse before the cart" paradox. Besides, in the proper context, born again and saved are synonymous terms (*same meaning*). A sinner has to first believe in Christ and then he is born again. The exercise of genuine faith (*repentance, an inherent part of true faith*) always comes **before** salvation. We don't get saved in order to obtain faith (*as Hyper-Calvinists claim*); we believe (*exercise faith*) in order to be saved (*Acts 16:30, 31*). The Holy Spirit quickens a sinner's conscience of his lost condition before he is saved. Sinners are convicted of their sin, but only a few that are convicted do get saved. If a sinner gets saved, he has acted upon repentance and faith.

(**NOTE: Arthur W. Pink** (1886-1952) infected many good men with the false doctrine of Hyper-Calvinism. Pink taught that one must be born again **before** trusting Christ. Pink does not say the Word of God, wielded by the Holy Spirit, produces saving faith; he said the new birth is the "cause" of faith. Untrue, the new birth is the "consequence" or result of exercised faith.

Actually, Arthur Pink flip-flopped on a lot of doctrines [from premillennial and dispensational to amillennialism]. At one time, he moved into **Theosophy** [an Eastern religion rejecting Judeo-Christian beliefs] and said fundamentalist leaders, like Arno C. Gaehelein, James M. Gray, and William L. Pettingill, were doing as much harm to the cause of Christ as the high priest of modernism, Harry Emerson Fosdick, and the higher critics.

Pink attended Moody Bible Institute six weeks and quit. He told the administrator that he was wasting his time. Pink died in Scotland in 1952, where he spent his last years without attending any church (*The Biblical Evangelist*, May-June, 2006, "Is a Sinner Made Alive Before Being Born Again?")

Arthur Pink, the hyper-Calvinist, says in his book (The Sovereignty of God), To argue that man is a free, moral agent and the determiner of his own destiny, and that therefore he has the power to checkmate his Maker, is to strip God of the attribute of omnipotence.

To the Hyper-Calvinists, this is tantamount to saying, that, if a man has a free will, God is not omnipotent or sovereign. The free will of men to choose can easily be proven by foolishly stepping in front of a moving Mack truck or jumping off a tall building. If God would allow a person the free will to do such a foolish thing, why would God refuse to allow a man to choose to obey the Gospel call to salvation rather than going to Hell for all eternity? It is plain to see that Hyper-Calvinists do not believe that men possess the freedom to trust in the Gospel of Christ for salvation. If it takes the absurd intellectual theology of Hyper-Calvinism to qualify for rightly dividing the word of truth, please spare this writer from the confusion of reformed theology.

Again, Arthur Pink (of Hyper-Calvinism) says in the same place that God "...is under no rule or law outside of His own will and nature..." (This is precisely the reason why man must have a free will; then, no one can accuse God of being a respecter of persons).

Hyper-Calvinists say, When God created the world, angels, and mankind, He determined that certain of the angels and all men would sin. God must have caused them to sin because He is sovereign and there is no will but His own. If a man is a free, moral agent, then God is not sovereign. Therefore God is the Author and direct cause of sin.

34

Now, the confused Calvinists blame God for sin. Their illogical dogmas deprive man of being a free, moral agent. If man had no will to choose to sin, then it is God that forced him to sin, according to extreme Calvinism. If man does not have a free will to choose, as Hyper-Calvinists claim, then it stands to reason that man cannot be held accountable for either believing or rejecting God's offer of salvation. That kind of extreme Calvinistic logic (*that God must have caused them to sin because He is sovereign),* puts the blame upon God. Even common sense tells you, if man is not a free, moral agent and cannot choose, he is not deserving of the punishment of Hell, nor is he deserving of the joys of Heaven. Man is never deserving of Heaven; actually, the only reason man is deserving of Heaven is because he chooses to believe (*free will*) in Christ's finished work on the cross of Calvary. All sins were charged to Christ, and Christ's righteousness was imputed to all that have trusted in Him. Christ died as the absolute perfect substitute (*vicariously*) for sin for ALL, for WHOSOEVER.

Hyper-Calvinists say, God sent His Son to Earth to redeem a limited number of men whom He chose to save. He chose to condemn the rest; they spend eternity in Hell **without even having a choice** in the matter of salvation. God professed that this plan of limited redemption was motivated by His love for the world.

To say that Christ died for all when He really died for just a limited few, or to invite all men to believe in Christ and be saved, when you know that they cannot believe, is both deceitful and cruel. God is not capable of either of these things.

Hyper-Calvinists say that God condemns men to the Lake of Fire to pay for sins that God made them commit and for rejecting salvation that God chose in eternity past not to give them. This false dogma is in double error: God hates sins and made no man to sin. If

35

man rejected salvation as Hyper-Calvinists claim, then man's rejection expresses choice.

God is not the author or cause of sin. God cannot be tempted with evil, neither tempteth he any man (*James 1:13*). God is holy. If God is holy (*and He is*), then man must be a free, moral agent who "chooses" to sin (*as Adam and Eve*). If man has no free will, then God willed him to sin and God would not be holy. To say that Christ died only for a few (when He died all), is not a genuine offer of salvation. God is just in condemning sinners to Hell because He neither caused their sin nor their unbelief. Man has a will and chooses to sin and reject God's offer of salvation. Calvinists sacrifice God's holiness, justice righteousness, truthfulness, and love, to maintain a false view of His sovereignty. God chose to save man by the death and resurrection of His Only Begotten Son. God offers salvation to ALL on the basis of repentance and faith alone. God's sovereignty and man's free will are in perfect harmony.

If man is as a puppet, without a will of his own in the matter of coming to Christ for salvation, then testing, temptation, obedience, and disobedience have no meaning or application in life. God did not force Abraham and Job to pass their extreme tests. God did not force Adam and Eve to sin and warned them in advance. Neither can the devil force you to sin. If man did not have a free will to sin, he could not have sinned and be judged guilty of Hell fire and everlasting judgment.

If Hyper-Calvinists refer to spiritual death of the unsaved as dead in trespasses and sins, then so were all men in like manner. If God only allowed certain ones to respond to the Gospel call to salvation, then the others could not be held accountable, seeing as how they "allegedly" could not respond. (*Again and again, Hyper-Calvinists claim that men are not able to respond*). Again and again, God is no respecter of persons. Man has always **resisted** the call of God to salvation. If man resisted, then he must have had a choice.

Election is taught in Scriptures and involves a choice of at least three things: 1) Choice of nations; 2) Choice of individuals to a particular action (*whether they are saved or unsaved*); 3) Choice of sinners to be the children of God (*disputed by Calvinists*).

God is sovereign

God is sovereign. God can and will do as He pleases, but He is also just and no respecter of persons (*Romans 2:11*).

Many questions can be proposed:

-QUESTION: Did God create some to be lost and some to be saved?

ANSWER: Absolutely Not! God is no respecter of persons. God could not designate or compel a man to do wrong without being a partaker of man's guilt; thereby, making Himself a sinning god. Neither could a holy God compel a man to always do right without taking away his personality and will.

QUESTION: Did God know certain ones would be lost when He gave them life?

ANSWER: Yes! God, through His foreknowledge and omniscience, foreknew who would be lost, but that did not prevent Him from creating man for His own purpose (*Ephesians 1:4-5, 9, 19; 2:7; 3:11; 5:27*). God had already provided the means of salvation before He created man. Golgotha was not an afterthought to God.

By using the sovereignty of God in an inappropriate application to bolster their false view of election and predestination, the extreme Calvinists teach that God predestines men to Hell or Heaven without any regard for their own will. To be sure, all men are destined either to

Heaven or Hell, but they do have a choice in the matter. Predestination is the exercise of God's will by which He brings to pass certain results, determined beforehand in Heaven, because of His omniscience. **Predestination has no application to salvation; it applies to the future lives and events of both the lost and saved.**

Scriptures plainly teach that all men are lost. God has chosen certain ones to be saved, but He has not limited that number; it is open to whosoever will. God rejects those that reject His way of salvation (*as Cain's unbloody sacrificial offering of the works of his hands - Genesis 4:5*). God saves those who receive His way of salvation (*as Abel's sacrificial blood offering - Genesis 4:4*). Salvation is a **gift** (*Romans 6:23; Ephesians 2:8*) through Jesus Christ alone (*John 14:6; I Timothy 2:5; Acts 4:12; I John 5:4, 5*). To be saved, a sinner must not only believe in their head (*devils do that*) but also believe the Gospel in their heart (*Romans 10:9-10, 13*). Calvinism's inability to reconcile the sovereignty of God with man's free will does not militate against the veracity of either ot the two doctrines.

The Hyper-Calvinist's flawed interpretation of election and predestination leads to a dead-end doctrine of fatalism, inability, and hopelessness. It is opposed to hope, mercy and salvation; it also denies that man has a choice. Without the power of choice, man cannot be held accountable for his sin, and neither can be charged for anything that befalls him.

(**Disclaimer:** The writer's critique of Hyper-Calvinism is not intended in any way as an attack upon the integrity of our Calvinist brethren (nor our Arminian brethren). Much of scholarly, and dependable biblical expositions are written by well qualified, gifted, and intelligent Presbyterians --- with the exception of Augustine's Hyper-Calvinism.)

Do not wait for an exposition of free will from our Hyper-Calvinist brethren.

It is wise to not become educated beyond your understanding.

Even Lucifer had a free will:

Isaiah 14:13: I will ascend into heaven; *14:13:* I will exalt my throne; 1*4:13:* I will sit also upon the mount; *14:14:* I will ascend above the heights; *14:14:* I will be like the most high.

Would God be just in giving Satan the power to attempt to destroy Israel and humanity itself, and not give sinners the way to escape? Would God be just in giving angels a free will to rebel against Him but deny those that are made in His very own image the choice of eternal glory?

In John 5:40, Jesus pleaded with unbelievers, Ye will not come to Me, that ye might have life. It is not that a sinner "cannot" come but they "will not" come. **Again and again, if they were unable to come, they could not be held accountable for their lost condition.** Actually, the inability of a sinner to choose would militate against the aspects of God's attributes of holiness, long suffering, mercy, grace, and love.

Election of Service is seen all throughout the Bible:

- God chose Abel instead of Cain (Why? Cain chose an unbloody sacrifice; Abel chose God's prescribed blood sacrifice).

- God chose Shem instead of Ham and Japheth.

- God chose the crafty conniver, Jacob, instead of Esau.

- God chose Ephraim, the younger, over Manasseh the elder.

- God chose Joseph over his older brethren.

- God chose David over his older brethren.

- God chose the nation of Israel (Isaiah 45:4), though there were seven greater nations.

- God chose the Church as a spiritual institution (after judicial Israel failed -(Ephesians 1:4).However, the NT Church does not replace Israel (false "Replacement Theology").God is not finished with Israel, and she has a glorious future after Daniel's 70th Week of Prophecy (Jacob's Time of Trouble – Jeremiah 30:7; the Tribulation Period).

Brother Shelton Smith (editor of *The Sword of the Lord* newspaper) is convinced that Election and Predestination has nothing to do with salvation but concerns sanctification of a saved person. Below is a brief excerpt concerning election and predestination from Dr. Shelton's message that appeared in The Sword of the Lord newspaper:

> *"For whom he did foreknow, he also did predestinate to be conformed to the image of his Son."—Rom. 8:29.*

What is God's intent, His design and purpose for us? When He saves us, He intends via "His workmanship" (Ephesians 2:10) to mold us into the likeness of Christ, according to verse 29 of Romans 8.

So the predestinating that God did was not about who would be saved, but about what He had determined to do with those who did get saved. In other words, predestination is about sanctification, not salvation!

You can easily confirm this with the Ephesians passage:

"According as He hath chosen us in Him before the foundation of the world, that we should be holy and without blame before Him in love."—Ephesians 1:4

Ephesians 1:4 says, He hath chosen us *(eklogo)*. That is, He made a decision before the foundation of the world in regard to us. His decision was that we should be holy and without blame before Him. Again, the text clearly indicates that what was predestinated was sanctification (not salvation). Once you are saved, the Lord intends to work on you, perfecting you and maturing you until you look like what He wants you to be (*The Sword of the Lord,* October 1, 2010, pp. 1, 16, 17).

Before the foundation of the world (*2 Timothy 1:9; Ephesians 1:4*), believers were chosen: **to Adoption** (*Ephesians 1:5*); **to children of God** (*Romans 8:16, 17*); **to Good works** (*Ephesians 2:10*); **to Conformity to Christ** (*Romans 8:29*); t**o Escape from delusions of antichrist** (*2 Thessalonians 2:13*); **to Sons of God** (*Romans 8:14*); **to Eternal glory** (*Romans 9:23*).

In his booklet, TULIP, Curtis Hutson says, "Vic Lockman attempts to prove the five points of Calvinism. Under the point, Unconditional Election, he quotes Ephesians 1:4, but he only quotes the first part of the verse: "He hath chosen us in him before the foundation of the world." However, that is not the end of the verse. Mr. Lockman, like most Calvinists, stopped in the middle of the verse. The entire verse reads; "According as He hath **chosen us** in Him before the foundation of the world, t**hat we should be holy** and without blame before Him in love." The verse says nothing about being chosen for Heaven or Hell. It says we are chosen that we should be holy and without blame before Him in love."

Lockman also quotes **John 15:16**, "Ye have not chosen Me, but I have chosen you..."Again, he stops in the middle of the verse,"...and ordained you that ye should go and bring forth fruit, and that your fruit should

41

remain: that whatsoever ye shall ask of the Father in My name, he may give it you." This verse says nothing about being chosen for Heaven or Hell. It says we are **chosen to go and bring forth fruit,** a soul winner (Proverbs 11:30).

Simply speaking, the **elect** are **predestined** unto the adoption of children and also **to be conformed to the image of His Son**; this is according to the **foreknowledge** of God – (I Peter 1:2; Ephesians 1:4-5, 11; Romans 8:29-30; Philippians 3:21).

In simple terminology, it is predetermined by God that the saved are destined to receive the adoption of children and ultimately blessed with a glorified body like unto the Son of God. In this new celestial glorified body like unto Christ's body, the saints of God will be conformed to the image of His Son. They will have a mind, heart, and soul "one" with Christ.

> Romans 8:29: For whom He did foreknow, He also **did predestinate to be conformed to the image of His Son**, that He might be the firstborn among many brethren.

In this verse of Romans 8:29, predestination of a saint concerns the believer's future likeness to Christ (*I John 3:2*). The Hyper-Calvinist view of predestination is twisted to say that salvation itself is predestinated, not conformity to Christ. Intellect can be a great asset, but alone it is insufficient for spiritual prowess and a deeper degree of spiritual truth. As far as the intellect is concerned, most of the false cults were begun by very intelligent people who were spiritual ignoramuses. It is the spiritual man of the heart that should rule believers (*Romans 10:9, 10: I Corinthians 2:14-16*).

The writer very definitely believes in **the sovereignty of God** (*Romans chapters 9-11*), but the sovereignty of God does not rob men of their will to choose. It is God Himself who invites whosoever will (*John 1:9; 3:16; 6:51; Acts 10:43; Romans 10:13; 11:32; I Timothy 2:4, 6; 4:10; Hebrews 2:9; 2 Peter 3:9; I John 2:2; 4:14; Revelation 22:17).* Nowhere in Scriptures is it said of salvation, Only the elect need apply. Again, the elect speaks of those who are already saved.

If predestined to Hell or Heaven without a will to choose is accurate theology, then whosoever will would necessarily have to be a false invitation to salvation. Both cannot be correct since they are in opposition with one another. There is not a single verse or text in the Bible that says a person is predestined to Heaven or Hell, without their choice.

In order to bolster their false view of election, the extreme Calvinists will emphasize the number of times that the words election, predestination, and ordain, occur in Scriptures. They reckon that the number of occurrences justifies their private theology. In striking contrast, Hyper-Calvinists never attempt to answer the numerous explicit invitations for all, whosoever will, and the whole world, to accept salvation. Jesus gave Himself a ransom **for all** (*2 Corinthians 5:14, 15; I Timothy 2:4, 6; 4:10; 2 Peter 3:9; Acts 10:43*).

Even some Baptists have been carried away with the false dogma of Hyper-Calvinism:

(Viz., Two-Seed-in-the Spirit Predestinarian Baptist; Reformed Baptist; United Baptists which has both Calvinistic and Arminian believers; some Southern Baptists).

Hyper-Calvinists argue that if Jesus died for the whole world (*and He did*), the whole world would be saved. The death of Jesus Christ on the cross was sufficient for **all**, but it is efficient only to those who freely put their trust in God's mercy and grace.

43

Calvinists conveniently overlook the historical fact that extreme Calvinism originated with the brilliant Catholic priest, Augustine, and eventually siphoned down through the Protestant ranks to latter day Hyper-Calvinists (*Viz., John Calvin; Martin Luther; Arthur Pink; Loraine Boettner; John Piper; James Kennedy; B. B. Warfield; Samuel Rutherford; V. Lockman; Herman Hoeksema; et al*).

(NOTE: Bible believing Baptists are **not** Protestant. Baptists were never in the Roman Catholic Church; consequently, they never came out of it, and are not Protestants. Study church history.)

> *John 1:12: But **as many as received Him**, to them gave He power to become the sons of God, even to them that believe on His name.*

Believing and Receiving (*faith*) is the determining factor of salvation. Believing is an act of the will (*freedom of choice*).

Thessalonian believers chosen to salvation:

> *2 Thessalonians 2:13-14: But we are bound to give thanks alway to God for you, brethren beloved of the Lord, because God hath from the beginning **chosen you to salvation through sanctification of the Spirit and belief of the truth**: Whereunto He called you by our gospel, to the obtaining of the glory of our Lord Jesus Christ.*

Observe the order: God **chose** the Thessalonians to salvation before they were born (*from the beginning*); then He **called** them, they heard the Gospel, **believed** the truth (*choice*), and were **sanctified** (*set apart*) by the Holy Spirit, eventually **destined** (*or predestined)* to be **glorified** in Christ (*Romans 8:30*) and **conformed** to His image (*Romans 8:29*). The Spirit used human messengers (*Acts 16:9*). However, of the many who were called of the Thessalonians, as Paul preached and taught, on*ly* some of them believed *(choice, Acts 17:4).*Many of Paul's listeners resisted *(free will)* the call and refused *(choice)* to believe. These were not chosen; Jesus said, "for many be **called**, but few [*are*] **chosen**" (*Matthew 20:16*).

Beginner Bible students learn very early an important method of interpreting Scriptures (*"hermeneutics"*). When Scriptures may appear contradictory, you always interpret the true meaning in the clear light of explicitly stated texts on the subject. You do not interpret a verse or text that is somewhat obscure and difficult to understand by referring to another passage that may not be not clear; neither do you interpret a passage simply because it appears to fit your private belief. To be rightly understood, difficult passages may require the study and prayer of mature, spiritual believers, comparing Scriptures to Scriptures. If students of the Bible cannot understand truth when it is expressly stated in Scriptures with words of elementary school level (*Viz., whosoever; all; the whole world; et al*), how can they expect to understand passages that may appear vague?

God's divine order is Foreknowledge, Election, and Predestination. The foreknown are elected and the elect are predestinated. The **elect** are comprised of whosoever will, and sadly, the **non-elect** are comprised by whosoever will not (*John 5:40*). The Elect body of God's children is composed of those believers who have put their faith in God's sacrificial offering for their sin. Jesus alone is God's offering for sin.

It is strange that in this brief, temporal stay on earth, men have the liberty to make all kinds of trivial choices that matter little and have no value in eternity, but at the same time, extreme religionists say God does not extend liberty for all to believe in Christ for salvation.

45

*Revelation 22:17: And the Spirit and the bride say, Come. And let him that heareth say, Come. And let him that is athirst come. And **whosoever** will, let him take the water of life freely.*

Whosoever will is so easy to understand that a fool, though a wayfaring man, shall not err therein (*Isaiah 35:8*). It is the highway of holiness.

*John 4:14: But **whosoever** drinketh of the water that I shall give him shall never thirst; but the water that I shall give him shall be in him a well of water springing up into everlasting life.*

Hyper-Calvinism History

The study of religious history reveals that Hyper-Calvinism was initiated by the Catholic priest, Augustine. Hyper-Calvinism was formally accepted by the Council of Orange in AD 529 and approved by Pope Boniface II.

The dogmas of Augustine and the writing of John Calvin's "*Institutes*" of Hyper-Calvinism, agree with the erroneous view labeled as "unpardonable reprobation." This view (*predestined to Hell*) is under the letter "T" of the acrostic TULIP (*Total Depravity*). Calvin taught Perseverance of the Saints (t*he "P" of TULIP*) and Augustine's sacramental salvation (*the belief that people could not receive God's grace unless they belonged to the church and received the sacraments of Baptism and the Lord's Supper*).

Actually, Augustine was erroneous in much of his theology. Augustine gave the Catholic Church (*Protestant churches followed)* the alien dogmas of infant Baptism; the error that un-baptized infants are damned; baptismal regeneration (for all); the error of a non-existent purgatory; the idea that the first resurrection is the new birth; and the worship of Mary. Certainly, no one can honestly accuse traditional, fundamental Baptists of believing these heresies. Augustine also held that the

Apocrypha is part of Scripture, and that the sin of Adam and Eve was sex (why did God instruct Adam and Noah to replenish the earth, if proper sex was sin?)

Augustine's study of neoplatonism (*the soul being capable of being reunited in trance or ecstasy to an indivisible being*) convinced him that God existed in the soul of every human being (*World Book Encycl.*, Vol. 1, p 860, Copyright © 1980, U.S.A.). That is the apostate philosophy of, "The Fatherhood of God and the Brotherhood of man." The unsaved are of their father, the devil (*John 8:44*).

Augustine's Teachings Contrary to Baptist Belief

Arminian brethren falsely accuse Baptist brethren of following after Augustine's teachings (*Augustine - 354-430*). Of course, this is not true. Augustine was the originator of Hyper-Calvinism and Baptists do not believe his erroneous dogmatism. Augustine's teachings were not in Baptist teachings, but they did appear in the writing of John Calvin, Martin Luther, Arthur Pink, Vick Lockman, Loraine Boettner and others. Even today, the teachings of Augustine's Hyper-Calvinism remain in Presbyterian, Lutheran, other Protestant churches, and Churches of Reformed Theology. (*If we digress into the history of Hyper-Calvinism, we find that its adherents were not kind to Separatist Christians, such as the Anabaptists, who were severely persecuted by Protestants.*)

Late in his life, Augustine came to a pessimistic view about original sin, grace, and predestination: the ultimate fates of humans, he decided, are predetermined by God in the sense that some people are granted divine grace to enter Heaven and others are not, and human actions and choices cannot explain the fates of individuals. This view was influential throughout the Middle Ages and became even more important during the

Reformation of the 16th century when it inspired the doctrine of predestination put forth by Protestant theologian, John Calvin – (*Microsoft ® Encarta ® Encyclopedia 2005* © 1993-2004 Microsoft Corporation).

According to an article in, *Prophecy In The New*s magazine (*August 2014, p. 10*), Augustine of Hippo, the theological doctor of the Roman Church, was a religious eclectic. He incorporated aspects of Persian **Manichaeanism** (*worship of angelic spirits*), **Buddhism** (*asceticism and universal consciousness*) and **neoplatonism** (*spiritualization of Christ*) into the formal church. He redefined salvation, not as relationship with God through Jesus Christ, but as conformity to the rule of the local church. He set the stage for **monasticism** and its accompanying variations of asceticism and celibacy. A new priesthood inserted itself between God and man. The illiterate plowman believed what he was told, with virtually no access to Latin Scriptures.

Primary Causes of Erroneous Dogmas and Doctrinal Differences Within the Church

➤ Taking Scriptural statements out of their proper context and/or failing to compare Scriptures with Scripture**...**

➤ Failing to rightly interpret grammatical constructions in the preserved Greek and Hebrew texts (as well as that of the English text)**...**

➤ By interpreting Scripture by human experience instead of understanding human experience by the Scripture**...**

➤ Denominational and religious pride**...**

➤ Influence and zeal of false prophets and dogmatism of phony teachers**...**

➢ The natural and carnal man cannot receive the things of God (*I Corinthians 2:14-15*)...

➢ Differences by carnal believers (*numerous in the church at Corinth*)...

➢ Believers unwilling to be guided by the Holy Spirit (*John 14:26; 16:13*)...

➢ Satanic attacks...

Due to Various Shades of Meanings, Many Greek Words Can Be Translated Into Numerous English Words.

Following are Examples:

✓ "Diakonos" is translated into **3 English words:** deacon; minister; and servant.

✓ "Anothen" is translated into **5 English words:** above; again; anew; first; top.(This is the word Jesus used to tell Nicodemus that he must be born again – John 3:7.)

✓ "Diakonia" is translated into **9 English words:** administration; minister; ministration; ministering; ministry; office; relief; service; serving.

✓ "Didomi" is translated into about **22 English words:** add; adventure; bestow; cause; commit; deliver; give; grant; make; minister; offer; power; put; receive; render; set; shew; smite; suffer; take; utter; yield.

✓ "Logos" is translated into about **25 English words:** account; cause; communication; do; doctrine; fame; intent; matter; mouth; preaching; question; reason; reckon; report; rumour; saying; show; speech; talk; thing; tidings; treatise; utterance; word; work.

✓ "Poieo" is translated into about **31 English words or word forms:** abide; appoint; bear; bring; cause; commit; continue; deal with; do; execute; exercise; fulfill; gain; give; hold; keep; make; mean; observe; ordain; perform; provide; purpose; put; shew; shoot forth; spend; take; tarry; work; yield.

✓ "Ginomai" is translated into about **39 English words or word forms**: arise; assemble; become; befall; behave; bring; come; continue; divide; do; end; fall; far; finish; follow; forbid; grow; have; keep; marry; means (by...of); ordain; pass; past; perform; place (take); prefer; prove; publish; shew; sound; spent; spring; take; turn; use; was; wax; work.

The context determines the word of best meaning. However, some Greek words, such as "aima," haima, (*hah' ee-mah*) can only be translated into **one** English word, **blood**, not "death" as some modern New Age English versions translate (*Good News Bible* for *example*).

THE ARMINIAN CHRISTIAN

The writer will use the term *Arminian* frequently throughout this writing. **Arminian** is a term named after Jacobus Arminius, a Dutch theologian [*1560-1609*] who wrote a remonstrance (document of reasoning) to counter the extreme views of Hyper-Calvinism (*as taught by Augustine and John Calvin*). Arminius rightly charged that Hyper-Calvinists teach an incorrect view of Bible predestination. Arminius believed (*correctly*) that the Gospel was for whosoever; however, Arminius taught (*incorrectly*) that salvation was conditional and men may relapse from a state of grace and die in their sins lost.

(**NOTE:** The great Protestant preacher, John Wesley, propagated Arminius' false dogma of Christians losing their salvation; John Calvin, the brilliant Protestant preacher, taught Augustine's erroneous dogma of people being predestinated to Hell or Heaven without having a will of their own. Even the **best** theologians and preachers can and do fall short.)

The writer is convinced that **Arminian** brethren insist upon the probability of a believer becoming unsaved in order to justify their private dogma of a *conditional or probationary* salvation. Most Arminians also believe in multiple salvations of the same person. They say that a saved person can become unsaved and afterwards become saved again. Arminianism is a form of "conditional" salvation that relies upon a person's good works and obedience for "allegedly" retaining their salvation. It appears to this writer that our Arminian brethren may be more anxious in protecting their private passion of a conditional salvation rather than defending the Biblical definition of *eternal life*. As previously stated, the term, Arminian, refers to the unbiblical doctrine that saved people may fall from the state of grace and again be destined to Hell. There are only two options concerning the duration of salvation; It is either a 100 % certainty that a saint is saved forever (*eternal life*) and destined to Heaven or it is a 100 % certainty that a saved person can become lost again and be destined to Hell. There is no half-way house, man-made purgatory, or limbo state (*neutral ground*), to offer a second chance to Heaven after death.

Full Assurance of Salvation

Our Arminian brethren do not believe that you can be assured of Heaven until you get there. Contrary to this unorthodox doctrine, the writer of the book of Hebrews desires that all believers show diligence to the saving of the soul with **full assurance to the end.**

> *Hebrews 6:11: And we desire that every one of you do shew the same diligence to the **full assurance of hope unto the end**.*

> *Hebrews 10:22: Let us draw near with a true heart **in full assurance** of faith, having our hearts sprinkled from an evil conscience, and our bodies washed with pure water.*

See also Isaiah 32:16; I Thessalonians 1:5**.**

If (*hypothetically*) the permanence of salvation is dependent upon the believer's good works outweighing their bad works, they (*or, we*) cannot have full assurance at all! "**...**there is none that doeth good, no, not one" (*Psalms 14:1; Romans 3:10-12*).None certainly includes the most spiritual believers.

The Apostle **Peter** was fully assured of the end of his salvation**:**

> *I Peter 1:9: Receiving **the end** of your faith, even the **salvation** of your souls.*

This verse is saying that faith has done its work, salvation is one eternal thing (*without end; permanent*), begun in this life, **kept during this life by the power of**

God (*Psalms 121:5; I Peter 1:5; Jude 1, 24*), **sealed by the Holy Spirit** (*Ephesians 1:13; 4:30; 2 Corinthians 1:22*), not interrupted by death, and continues to and through all eternity (*John 3:16*). Of course, Peter was not depending upon his own faithfulness. Actually, Peter repented of his own unfaithfulness in the matter of his thrice denial of Lord Jesus.

John wrote that we may KNOW that we have Eternal Life (*I John 5:13*):

If believers in Christ are unconvinced and uncertain of the gift of eternal life, neither can they have full assurance of salvation. These uncertain believers assume that their soul may be in jeopardy of being lost before they die. During a Bible discussion, the writer asked a brother of Arminian persuasion if he knew for sure that he was going to Heaven, and he replied in the affirmative. The writer then asked him why he was sure of Heaven. The Arminian brother replied that he knew he would go to Heaven because he would keep himself faithfully true and saved until the end (*his words, not the writer's*). The writer believed that this man was genuinely saved. Of course, this dogma, of a saved person keeping himself saved, is contradicted in Scriptures (*I Peter 1:5; Psalms 121:5; Ephesians 1:13; 4:30; 2 Corinthians 1:22*). The same grace that saves us is the same grace that keeps us. Full assurance in God's Word gives us full joy:

> *I John 1:4: And these things write we unto you, that your **joy may be full**.*

> *I John 2:20, 27**: But ye have an unction from the Holy One, and ye know all things. But **the anointing which ye have received of Him abideth in you**, and ye need not that any man teach you: but as **the same anointing teacheth you of all things**, and is truth, and is no lie, and even as it hath taught you, ye shall abide in Him.*

53

I John 5:11-13: And **this is the record**, *that God hath given to us* **eternal life**, *and this life is in His Son. He that hath the Son hath life; and he that hath not the Son of God hath not life. These things have I written unto you that believe on the name of the Son of God;* **that ye may know that ye have eternal life**, *and that ye may believe on the name of the Son of God.*

Again, what part of, **"...that ye may know that ye have eternal life.."** do our Arminian brethren question? The assurance of Heaven (*eternal life*) is needed here upon earth, not in Heaven. We now see through a glass darkly, but then, face to face.

If (*hypothetically*) the security of salvation is limited only to those saints that are in Heaven, we cannot have any assurance of it here upon earth and the joy of eternal life would be void (*I John 1:4*).

If (*hypothetically*) we could lose our salvation on earth (or in Heaven), we would only have temporary life, depending upon our own ability to hold out. That is not eternal life!

Eternal life is not tantamount (*equal in value or status*) to a probationary salvation that is conditioned upon good works or holding out. To say, You cannot be sure of Heaven until you get there, is a false humility and a denial of Scripture (*I John 5:13*). Having full assurance (*Hebrews 6:11*) of salvation is a wonderful blessing; it is like escaping the religious smog of insecurity and entering into the clear light of Eternal Life.

This writer would be miserable if salvation was dependent upon himself to remain saved.

Why would God allow a believer to have lesser assurance of his eternal existence (*eternal life*) than human government can guarantee us of contemporary legal rights?

54

Eternal Life is Eternal Security

The Scriptures promise eternal life to all repentant sinners who are willing to trust in Christ's sacrificial death on the Cross of Calvary. Any other form of life would be conditioned upon human works which would fail in the end. Actually, anyone fully depending upon their own goodness or good works would perish. Believers are not justified by human works or personal virtues for salvation (*Ephesians 2:8, 9; Galatians 2:16; Romans 4:4-6*); neither are believers maintained or kept by works (*I Peter 1:5; Psalms 121:5*). Believers are saved by faith alone (*Ephesians 2:8, 9),* and sealed by the Holy Spirit unto the day of redemption (*Ephesians 1:13; 4:30; 2 Corinthians 1:22*).

A Friend Excommunicated From Church

Years ago (*1970s*), the writer became acquainted with a man from a coal mining district of West Virginia. Jacob had gotten saved in his hometown and began preaching shortly afterwards. He could not read before he was saved, but in his zeal to study the Bible, he was able to learn to read very quickly. Jacob memorized much Scripture and would preach extemporaneously (*without notes*) on a moment's notice on any Bible text requested. Jacob told this writer that in his early days of salvation, he began preaching simple Bible verses of eternal life, quoting them exactly as they occurred In the KJV Bible (*Viz., John 3:16, 36; 5:24; Romans 6:23; et al)*. He was soon summoned before a council of angry church elders. The council wanted to know what books he had been reading, and where he gotten that eternal life doctrine. Jacob replied that he did not have any books, and he was "just preaching exactly what he read from the Bible."

Who Are Those That Draw Back Unto Perdition?

The writer of Hebrews (*the writer believes Paul*) says that he and fellow believers are **not of them who**

draw back unto perdition. Paraphrasing, this could be properly interpreted as saying, Believers of eternal life do not believe in becoming lost again and going to Hell.

> *Hebrews 10:39: But we are not of them who draw back unto **perdition**; but of them that believe to the **saving of the soul.***

The word "perdition" is from the Greek word "apoleia" (Strong's Greek #684) and the word occurs in the New Testament eight times (John 17:12; Philippians 1:28; 2 Thessalonians 2:3; I Timothy 6:9; Hebrews 10:39; 2 Peter 3:7; Revelation 17:8, 11).In each use, the wicked is referred to in the final state: **(Perdition synonyms:** Entire loss or ruin; utter loss of the soul; future misery or eternal death; damnation; loss; destruction; perishing.) The Greek word, apoleia, translated as perdition, is also translated as "destruction" (Matthew 7:13; Romans 9:22; Philippians 3:19; 2 Peter 2:1; 2 Peter 3:16). In the context of these references, destruction has the same meaning as perdition. The writer does not believe that Greek expositors are without error, but their knowledge and expertise of the Greek and Hebrew languages (and English) deserves a fair hearing. One Greek expositor says that the Greek word, apoleia, which is translated as both "perdition" and "destruction," means, "To destroy fully; the state after death wherein exclusion from salvation is a realized fact; the second death which is eternal exclusion from Christ's kingdom; etc." This same Greek expositor also lists **eternal life** as the "antonym" (opposite) of perdition. Eternal life has the same meaning and is synonymous with the security of the believer. In the context of their usage, **both perdition and destruction point to a lost man in his final state.** There is no doubt that perdition is the future lot of those excluded from the kingdom of God. In popular usage, men make the word perdition a synonym for Hell and eternal punishment.

The Jews frequently expressed a man's "destiny" by calling him the offspring of various entities with titles, such as, "The Son(s) of," "The Child of," "Children of, "et al -- <u>Examples</u>:

➢ CHILDREN: of Disobedience (Ephesians 2:2); of the resurrection (Luke 20:36); of God (Matthew 5:9); of that wicked one (Matthew 13:38); of Light (Luke 16:8); of the devil (I John 3:10); of this world (Luke 16:8); of the Highest (Luke 6:35); of Belial (Deuteronomy 13:13)

➢ DAUGHTER: of Belial (I Samuel 1:16)

➢ SON(S): of God (John 1:12; Romans 8:14; I John 3:1, 2); of Belial (Judges 19:22;

➢ I Samuel 2:12; 25:17; 2 Kings 21:10); of perdition.

➢ MAN (MEN): of God (Joshua 14:6; Judges 13:8; I Samuel 2:27; 2 Timothy 3:17); of Belial (I Samuel 25:25; 30:22; 2 Samuel 16:7; 20:1

➢ CHILD: of The Holy Ghost (Matthew 1:18); of Hell (Matthew 23:15); of the devil (Acts 13:10)

*Hebrews 10:39: But we are **not of them who draw back unto perdition**; but of them that believe to the saving of the soul.*

Believers in *eternal life* trust in and believe that the soul is secure in Christ.

Church Dropouts

The question arises (*rightly so*), What of those religious people who professed to know God, were baptized into the Church membership, served in a church position for a while, and then went back into a life of sin? The question should be, What do the Scriptures say about those who went out from among us?

John tells us of some that went out to their old life were "not all" genuine believers.

> *I John 2:19: They **went out** from us, but **they were not of us**; for if they had been of us, they would no doubt have continued with us: but they **went out**, that they might be made manifest that **they were not all of us**.*

The answer is clearly stated. These former outwardly reformed, religious people were merely false religious professors mingled among God's people for a season. Even today, many apostates (*formerly hidden in Christian Churches*) are now coming out of the closet and are attempting to sanitize sinful behaviour. Many apostates even openly deny the deity of Christ and Bible miracles. This is the spirit of antichrist and apostate scoffers working in the last days (*I John 2:18-19; 2 John 7-9; 2 Peter 2:1-2; 2 Timothy 3:5-7*).

<u>Of course, Jesus knew the real condition of these people:</u>

> *John 6:64: But there are some of you that believe not. For Jesus knew from the beginning who they were that believed not, and who should betray Him.*

Jesus knew from the beginning that Judas was not a true believer. Jesus was referring to unbelievers within religious circles of believers, not to rank and file sinners on the outside. These false professors maintained a religious profession for a while. Jesus makes a clear statement of fact that some of His own disciples believed not. Two verses later, the Scriptures say, From that time many of **His disciples** went back, and walked no more with Him (*John 6:66*). Actually, a person would have to be very naive to believe that every religious person claiming to be saved is truly a born again Christian. Satan always has his counterfeits among God's people. These tares (*church players; stage actors; counterfeits;*

pretenders of the real) among the wheat, are unsaved religious people who merely resemble genuine saints on the outside. Again, tares resemble wheat in the blade stage, but they are discovered as enemy counterfeits in the fruit stage. "For every tree is known by his own fruit..." (*Luke 6:44*).

Our Arminian brethren may simply dismiss people who go out from the church as saved people who became lost again, but according to the Scriptures above (*John 6:64-66*), this is not always the case. Jesus knew from the beginning that there were those that believed not. These unsaved tares (*religious pretenders*) blended into the wheat (*body of true believers)* and were indistinguishable for a season, and then went out. There are many unsaved people in churches today that are mere **professors,** not **possessors**. These people (*I John 2:19; John 6:64*) went out that they might be made manifest that **they were not all of us**? A grasp of hermeneutics (*principles of Bible interpretation*) is not needed in order to understand this text.

When the Plain Sense of Scriptures Make Common Sense, Seek No Other Sense - (author unknown).

Professors and imitators have always plagued true religion. However, some genuine Christians also go out and separate themselves from among the brethren for a while. If they are truly born again, it is certain that **all** of them will be chastened of the Lord (*Hebrews 12:5-8*) and if they do not respond to the Lord's chastening, they may commit "a sin unto death" (*Romans 6:16; I John 5:16*).

Three Kinds of Believers

Babes: Babes in Christ have not grown to maturity from their spiritual infancy and their testimony (*and doctrine*) may be weak and questionable. Babes in Christ,

59

as well as carnal believers, can only feed upon milk, not upon the meat of the Word (*I Corinthians 3:1-3; Hebrews 5:12*).

Carnal: Carnal believers may live in such a worldly fashion as to make it difficult to distinguish them from the unsaved. Carnal believers are those who have been saved a sufficient length of time for growth *(Romans 8:7; I Corinthians 3:1-4; Hebrews 5:12),* but instead walk in the flesh as men.

Spiritual: The spiritual man has grown to maturity and has the mind of Christ. He judgeth all things, yet he himself is judged of no man (*I Corinthians 2:15; John 7:24*).

Presumptuous Willful Sinning

There are those deluded perfectionists that do not believe that a genuine believer can willfully sin. There are many instances in Scriptures that demonstrate presumptuous and willful sins of believers (*in contrast to stumbling inadvertently into sin*).

Bible Saints Who Sinned Willfully:

- **-Abraham** willfully sinned when he lied, denying that Sarah was his wife.

- **-Isaac** willfully sinned when he lied, as Abraham had done, and denied his wife.

- -**David** willfully sinned when he committed adultery with Bathsheba and ordered the murder of Bathsheba's husband.

- -**Peter** willfully sinned when he lied and denied Jesus; Peter even cursed.

None of these sinning brethren lost their salvation; neither is there any record of a second or a third spiritual birth.

If (*hypothetically*) a saved person could become unsaved and **if** (*hypothetically*) he could be saved the second time, Christ would have to be crucified over again. That will never happen! Christ died ONCE for sin and NOMORE (*Romans 6:10; Hebrews 9:12*).

The writer believes that most Christians are lacking in spiritual growth and prone to remain babes in Christ or to live in a carnal lifestyle. If the reader thinks this statement is exaggerated, check to see how much time most Christians spend watching TV versus reading the Bible (*also time in prayer and witnessing*). Probably, sins of omission are far greater than sins of commission among Christians. Of course Christians do sin presumptuously, but the children of God have an advocate with the Father, Jesus Christ, the Righteous:

> *I John 2:1-2:* **My little children** *these things write I unto you, that ye sin not. And if any man sin, we have an Advocate with the Father, Jesus Christ the righteous. And He is the propitiation for our sins: and not for ours only, but also for the sins of the* **whole world***.*

Antinomianism

Lest the reader misunderstands, Christianity is **not** a sinning religion of easy believe-ism (*antinomianism). True Christians cannot sin (*I John 3:9*) or cannot continue to practice a lifestyle of rebellion and iniquity. However, the Christian is not without sin in the absolute sense (*I John 1:8, 10; I John 2:1-2*). The carnal (*fleshly*) nature of the believer has **not** been eradicated (*cancelled; abrogated; done away with*). Even mental sin is condemned by Christ (*Matthew 5:28*). Believers cannot sin (*I John 3:9*) in the sense of becoming unsaved because God's seed (*John 14; 16, 17; 16:7, 13*) remains in them, and Christ's righteousness is imputed to them.

61

(*__Antinomianism:__ Antinomians erroneously state, Since there is the absence of the Law of Moses in the present Day of Grace, great latitude of conduct is permitted, and because of the liberty that believers have in the Dispensation of Grace, right conduct is unnecessary for living the Christian life after salvation.)

Babes in Christ, as well as carnal Christians, are absolutely justified for Heaven; they are just as secure in salvation, as mature, spiritual Christians. The most illiterate, carnal babe is **in grace** just as much as the most spiritual believer. Again, there **is** a difference between the believer's state of daily walking (*fellowship and communion with God*) and that of his standing (*his salvation **in** Christ Jesus*). Jesus will confirm us unto the end that we may be blameless. He will not suffer His faithful to fail (*I Corinthians 1:7-8; Psalms 89:33*).

Christians Without Assurance of Heaven

It is undoubtedly true that many Christians do not have full assurance that they are going to Heaven. The greatest reason they do not have full assurance of Heaven is because they do not fully submit to the truth of Scriptures (*I John 5:11-13*). Most Christians are Arminian in their doctrine and teach that salvation is conditioned upon maintaining a certain degree of good works or faithfulness. This is the same as depending upon one's own good works for retaining salvation. Of course, a level of good works or the Nth degree of faithfulness required to "allegedly" remain saved has never been established by the Bible (*nor anyone else*). Most Arminian brethren will answer that God knows when your faithfulness or works comes short of keeping your salvation. This is the same as saying that a believer cannot have the assurance of Heaven while upon earth. This anemic perception of grace does not impart virtue nor the assurance of Heaven for the believer. Good works cannot keep us because good works did not save us. The same grace that saved us is the same grace that keeps us. Salvation is not faith plus works (*Galatians 2:16, 21; Ephesians 2:8, 9; Romans 4:4-6; 6:23*).

The believer can "know" (*I John 5:13*) that eternal life presently abides within. Our Arminian brethren say that no one can know for certain that they are going to Heaven until they get there. This is certainly a **fear-based perception** of everlasting life.

> *"...fear hath torment. He that **feareth** is not made perfect in love" (I John 4:18).*

Due to building repairs on this writer's home church, he attended a nearby Wesleyan Church service on a Wednesday evening (the writer has always loved the spirit of camp-meeting style Methodists). During the service, a lady stood up to testify and requested the Church to pray that she would hold out to the end and make it into Heaven one day (*her exact words*). The writer did not question the virtue of this lady nor her salvation and hope of Heaven, but he sure disagreed with her perception of everlasting life *(not intended as a negative slur upon the genuine integrity of many godly Arminian saints)*. However, salvation is not a hope so, think so, or maybe so, promise; eternal life is an absolute "know so" condition of the soul (*I John 3:2; 5:11-13; Ecclesiastes 3:14; John 10:27-29; I Peter 1:9; Hebrews 6:11*).

C. F. Baker says, Is our security a keeping of ourselves or of our acts merely? It is the flesh in the believer that causes all of his sins and failures, a part of the believer, the carnal nature. If the security God offers to us protects us only against some of the acts of our old nature and not against the nature itself, it is in effect no security at all.

The *new man* after God in the believer is created in righteousness and true holiness (*Ephesians 4:24;*

Colossians 3:10; 2 Peter 1:4). We will have to contend with the old man (*Adamic nature; sinful flesh*) as long as we are in this mortal body. At the First Resurrection (*I Corinthians 15:54*), the old nature will be eradicated. If the *new man* could reject Christ after having received Him in this life, he could do it also in the life to come. Paul committed **his soul** to God and was persuaded that He was able to keep it against that day.

> *2 Timothy 1:12: "...for **I know** whom I have believed and **am persuaded that He is able to keep** that which I have committed unto Him against that day."*

We can have full assurance of Heaven **if** we believe the word of God. **If** we do not take God at His Word, there is lack of trust; uncertainty, doubt, and fear may rule the day.

Again, our Arminian brethren believe (*correctly*) that believers are saved wholly by the grace of God, but believe (*incorrectly*) that believers are *kept* saved by their own faithfulness and good works. If a person is not kept by the power of God (*I Peter 1:5*), the only alternative is to be kept by their own power, or by some other entity. A saved person certainly is not kept saved by the power of Satan, nor angels, good or bad! Neither is a saved person kept saved by attempting to mix good works with God's grace.

> *Romans 11:6: And **if by grace, then is it no more of works**: otherwise grace is no more grace. **But if it be of works, then is it no more grace:** otherwise work is no more work.*

If Arminian brethren have truly trusted Christ as their Lord and Savior, they are justified and secure in God's salvation. They are assured of Heaven in spite of their private doctrine that advocates the possibility of losing salvation. The writer has confidence in Arminian brethren, despite our difference in the definition of eternal life.

Works of Self-Righteousness Doom Sinners

False religionists claim that they are going to Heaven by good works (*Proverbs 14:12*). However, they have been beguiled by Satan (*I Peter 5:8*), and they are following the spirit of error (*I John 4:6*). Those trusting upon their own righteousness to obtain salvation are entering through the wide gate that is the broad way to destruction (*Matthew 7:13*). All of their righteous deeds (*good works*) are as filthy rags in the sight of God (*Isaiah 64:6*).

> *Titus 3:5:* **Not by works of righteousness which we have done**, *but according to His* **mercy** *He saved us, by the washing of regeneration and renewing of the Holy Ghost.*

> *Galatians 2:16: Knowing that* **a man is not justified by the works of the law**, *but by the* f**aith** *of Jesus Christ, even we have believed in Jesus Christ, that we might be justified by the* f**aith** *of Christ, and not by the works of the law: for* **by the works of the law shall no flesh be justified**.

Things That Cannot Obtain Salvation

➤ Treating your fellow man right (*does not save*; *even the heathen do that*).

➤ Trusting in "so called" sacraments which is actually, Sacramental Salvation. (*Sacraments "so called" do not save; the only act that remits sin is, by faith, trusting the shed blood of Jesus Christ - Eph. 2:8; Heb. 9:22; Rev. 1:5*).

➤ Confessing sins to a priest (*does not save; there is only ONE Mediator*

➤ *between God and man, JESUS (I Timothy 2:5; Acts 4:12; John 14:6).*

65

- ➢ Trusting in good works outweighing bad works (*good works do not save - Titus 3:5; Romans 4:4-6; Ephesians 2:8-9);* all of our good works are as filthy rags *(Isaiah 64:6; Titus 3:5; Romans 3:10, 21-22).*

- ➢ Trusting in church authority (*does not save; the Bible is the only authority*).

- ➢ Partaking of communion (*does not save; Communion is an ordinance in remembrance of Christ's sacrificial death till he come (I Corinthians 11:23-26). Communion is given to those to observe who are **already** believers.*

- ➢ Learning catechism (*does not save; faith in Christ's propitiation saves, not learning*).

- ➢ Church Confirmation (*does not save; the Holy Spirit confirms us*).

- ➢ Being baptized (*does not save; water baptism is an ordinance whereby the believer publicly identifies with Christ's death, burial and resurrection in baptismal waters - I Corinthians 15:1-4; Galatians 2:20).*

- ➢ Church membership (*does not save; many unsaved people are church members*).

- ➢ Helping the poor which is commanded, commendable, and noble (*does not save; even the unsaved have mercy on the poor*).

- ➢ Being sincere (*does not save; many members of pagan religions are sincere. -Radical Muslims prove their sincerity by their jihad suicidal bombings as did the*

- ➢ *Japanese dive bombers of the hari kari Japanese cult of World War II*).

➤ Paying your dutiful debts (*does not save; only Christ could pay the sin-debt*).

➤ Living a good life (*does not save; no one can live holy or well enough (Psalms 14:1; Ecclesiastes 7:20; Romans 3:12*).

➤ Paying tithes (*does not save; the **unsaved** Pharisees paid tithe of all*).

➤ Doing penance (*does not save; penance is an invention of man). The sacrifice of a genuine **penitent heart** is required, Luke 13:3, 5, not self-atoning works*).

Some of these things are commendable, some are in error, and others may be ordered of the Lord; however, **none of these things nor a combination of these have any saving grace**. The very foundation **of false religion** is based upon good works combined with **sacerdotal** functions (*priestly mediators*).**Obedience to rituals and ordinances does not save nor retain salvation (**rituals were a large part to OT sacrificial offerings).

A religious dogma that dictates a dependence upon works to **obtain** salvation makes it a works salvation. Saints are Christ's workmanship (*Ephesians 2:10)* **after** they are saved. No one is saved by their works. Again, one of the most common errors of religion is the failure to distinguish between **works** and **faith,** for salvation (*Romans 11:6; Galatians 3:3)*. We are saved by grace through faith in the Saviour's finished work.

> *Romans 11:6: And* ***if by grace****, then it is* ***no more of works****: otherwise grace is no more grace. But if it be of works, then is it no more grace: otherwise work is no more work.*

True Bible salvation begins when Hell-deserving, broken-hearted sinners come to God in genuine repentance and **faith (***saving faith includes repentance – Luke 13:3; 18:3; Ephesians 2:8, 9*). Jesus Christ alone is the only way to God for salvation (*John 8:36; 14:6, 7; I Timothy 2:5; Acts 4:12*).If a sinner has any hope of Heaven, he must experience the **new birth** that is from above. Jesus made this plain to the unsaved, religious Jew, Nicodemus. Nicodemus was a Pharisee, and member of the Sanhedrin, the seventy-member, Jewish ruling body; he was also an unsaved member of the Jewish synagogue. This is much like **unsaved** church members during the church age (*John 3:1-12*).

If anyone could qualify for Heaven by observing the letter of the Law and clean outward living, surely the strict law-abiding leaders of the Pharisees would. However, self-righteousness and outward clean living cannot merit salvation.

> *Matthew 5:20: For I say unto you, That except your righteousness shall exceed the righteousness of the scribes and Pharisees, ye shall in no case enter into the kingdom of Heaven.*

The **new birth** (*spiritual birth*) is the **only way** of entering God's kingdom of redeemed people (*John 1:12; 3:3-7, 16, 18, 36*).

> *John 3:3: Jesus answered and said unto him (Nicodemus), Verily, verily, I say unto thee, Except a man be* **born again***, he cannot see the kingdom of God.*

> *John 3:7: Marvel not that I said unto thee,* **Ye (all) must be born again***.*

> *I Peter 1:23: Being* **born again***, not of corruptible seed (flesh), but of incorruptible (spiritual),* **by the Word of God***, which liveth and abideth for ever.*

> *Romans 10:17: So then* **faith** *cometh by hearing, and hearing by the* **Word of God***.*

> *Ephesians 2:8: For **by grace** are ye (all; everybody) saved through **faith**; and that not of yourselves: it is the **gift** of God.*

> *Matthew 18:3: And (Jesus) said, Verily I say unto you, Except **ye** (all) be converted, and become as little children, ye shall not enter into the kingdom of Heaven.*

The carnal ideas of men are not important. The Bible is the final authority in all matters (John 3:3-7; John 7:24; Matthew 7:19, 21-23; I Corinthians 6:2-3; Romans 3:20, 28; 4:4-6; Galatians 2:16, 21; 3:10).

Is it Presumptuous to Believe in Eternal Life?

It is NOT presumptuous to believe in eternal life. God expects His children to trust in His Word and be presumptuous in believing His promises. There is **fear** in an imperfect love that does not fully trust God's promises; perfect love casteth out fear (*I John 4:18*). The writer believes that the all-knowing (*omniscient)* God can give His children peace and absolute assurance of their *everlasting life,* **before** they get to Heaven. Of course, those that have assurance of Heaven are accused by Arminian brethren of being too presumptuous toward God. It is **not** presumptuous to take God at His Word. If we cannot trust God's Word and His promises, in whose words or promises can we trust?

> *"...**I give** unto them eternal life and **they shall never perish**, neither shall any man* (entity; power) *pluck them out of My hand" (John 10:28).*

> *"**All** that the Father giveth Me shall come to Me; and him that cometh to Me **I will in no wise cast out"** (John 6:37).*

It is not, I will give, if they hold out to the end. The word give of John 10:28 is a perfect present tense verb and expresses future continuance. Eternal means without end. Again, what part of eternal life or everlasting life do

69

our Arminian brethren not comprehend? If words do not convey exact meanings, we cannot conclude anything to be absolute. Eternal life majestically shouts future glorious life without end. Eternal life is not conditioned upon the believer's perseverance or performance. Biblically speaking, those who are not presumptuous enough to believe Scripture, are **doubting God's Word** (*John 1:45; 5:45-47; 10:28*). It is a very dangerous thing to doubt God's Word.

> *Romans 14:23: And* **he that doubteth is damned** *if he eat, because he eateth not of faith: for* **whatsoever is not of faith is sin***.*

God magnifies His Word above His own name - (*Psalms 138:2*).

We are admonished to be presumptuous about believing God's Word and to come boldly (*not arrogantly*) before God's Throne of Grace (*Hebrews 4:16*). Doubting the promise of the gift of eternal life is the same as doubting God's Word. The saints of God are also kept by the power of God (*I Peter 1:5; Psalms 121:5*).

Do Christians Sin?

As previously stated, Christians do **knowingly** sin. In the OT, there was even a sacrifice provided for those who sinned through ignorance (unknowingly).

By God's grace, saved people have an absolutely perfect **Advocate** (JESUS), who is interceding for all believers at the right hand of His Father. Jesus has never lost a single case and never will.

(**Advocate:** attorney; lawyer; mouthpiece; intercessor pleading the cause for another.)

> *I John 2:1-2:* **My little children***, these things write I unto you, that ye sin not. And* **if any man sin,** *we have an* **Advocate** *with the Father, Jesus Christ the righteous: And He is the propitiation for our*

70

sins: and not for ours only, but also for the sins of the whole world.

The believer's two Advocates:

One within: **The Holy Spirit**, that we might not sin (*John 16:18; I John 3:9*).

One above: **Jesus Christ**, if we should sin (*I John 2:1*)

There are **saved** people who sin both by **commission** (*I John 2:1*) and **omission** (*James 4:17*). Probably, sins of omission are the most frequent sins of believers. Even the apostle Paul conceded that **sin dwelt in his flesh** (*Romans 7:14-25*). Paul put his **body** in subjection daily. If Paul had sin abiding in his **flesh**, it is certain that all other Christians also have sin abiding in their flesh. The **sinful, carnal nature** of man has **not** been eradicated (*done away with; abolished*). Saved people are free from the **power** of sin, the **guilt** of sin, and the eternal **penalty** of sin, but they are not free from the **presence** nor the temptation and **commission** of sin (one glorious day, believers will be saved from the very presence of sin). Believers have **two natures**, the spiritual (*called divine nature*

2 Peter 1:4) and the Adamic nature (*sinful; physical; flesh - Romans 8:8*). The sin nature has not been done away with; if it were, there would be an absence of the trial or temptation of sin itself. Again, one future day, this body of sin (*Romans 6:6*) will be translated into a glorified spiritual body without sin (*I Corinthians 15:42, 44, 49, 53*).

Actually, the very fact that the God of the Bible anticipates the sins and failures of a Christian, demonstrates that He has also made provision for them. This is solid proof that eternal life does not depend upon the Christian's works and spiritual stamina (*I John 1:7, 9; 2:1*).

71

There are many classes of Christians (*Viz., good; bad; babes; carnal; obedient; disobedient; spiritual; et al*), but they are **all** children of God. Again, if disobedient believers continue to commit sin and do not respond to the chastening of the Lord, they may commit a sin unto death (*Romans 6:16; I John 5:16*).

A story of a secular nature may serve to illustrate (*as a parable*) the attributes and devotional levels of Christians. A very proficient, hardworking employee asked his supervisor why he did not make more money than his fellow employees, who did much less work. The supervisor told the hardworking employee that there were three kinds of employees that were paid the same rate. The first employee does just enough to hold his job, and no more. The second employee did his job fully, but did no extra. The third employee did his job well, and also went beyond the demands and did it better than what was expected of him. Yet all three made the same pay. This may serve to remind believers of the different commitment levels of Christians that are ALL going to Heaven, the same way, through the grace of God. Though no one can work for salvation and none deserve the joys of Heaven, they all are equal at the foot of the Cross.

<u>Although sin is always sin, there are different forms</u>

There are **sins of Commission** (*I John 3:4, 5; Romans 3:12*); **sins of Omission** (*James 4:17; Romans 7:19; I John 3:10*); **sins of Ignorance (***James 2:10; Numbers 19:11-13; Luke 11:14*); **sins of Nature** (*Romans 7:20, 21* - sins of nature are inherited through Adam's disobedience and the resultant sin curse passed upon all men - Romans 5:12; **sins of Presumption** (*Psalms 19:13; 2 Peter 2:10*); **sins of Rebellion** (I Samuel 15:23; Jeremiah 28:16)

As there are different forms of sins, there are also different grades of sin; some sins are greater than others (*even one sin is enough to condemn a sinner*). Jesus rated (*graded*) sin when He told Pilate that the one who delivered Him to Pilate had the greater sin: If there is a greater sin, there must be a lesser sin.

> *John 19:11: Jesus answered, Thou (Pilate) couldest have no power at all against Me, except it were given thee from above: therefore he that delivered Me unto thee hath **the greater sin**.*

Even Pilate could have repented of his terrible sin **if** he would have. God provided a remedy for all kinds of sin, that we might be made the righteousness of God in him.

Two Kinds of Sinning Saints:

There is a saint who is striving to live a holy life even though he/she may fall short of the glory of God(*Romans 3:9-12; Psalms 143:2; Isaiah 64:6; Philippians 1:27; Colossians 1:29; I John 1:8; 2:1-2*).

There is another saint who is carnal, out of fellowship, and may be living in a worldly fashion of sin (*I Corinthians 3:15; 5:5*).

From the outward appearance, it can be difficult to distinguish between a carnal, backslid believer (*I Corinthians 3:1-4*), and an unsaved church member who may be living a clean outward (external) pharisaical life.

> *Galatians 6:7: Be not deceived; God is not mocked: for whatsoever a man soweth that shall he also reap.*

If a person sows to the flesh, he shall reap corruption. If a person sows to the Spirit, he shall of the Spirit reap life everlasting (*Galatians 6:8*).

A Christian That Persists in His Sin

As stated several times earlier in this writing, if a sinning saint **refuses** to confess and forsake his sin when

73

he is chastened of the Lord, God may call him home by an untimely, premature death. There is a sin unto death for the believer.

> *I John 5:16-17: If any man see his brother sin a sin which is not unto death, he shall ask, and he shall give him life for them that sin not unto death.* **There is a sin unto death:** *I do not say that he shall pray for it. All unrighteousness is sin: and there is a sin not unto death.* (See Romans 6:16; I Corinthians 3:15; 5:5.)

The Scriptures are clear; God chastens His earthly children even as an earthly father should (*Hebrews 12:7, 9*). God may choose to deliver a disobedient believer to an untimely death when He deems it necessary or profitable. Of course, the earthly father is not expected to kill his son for disobedience. However, earthly fathers should be obedient in matters of civil law and corporal offenses (*Genesis 9:6; Exodus 21:12; Leviticus 24:21: Romans 13:1-7*).

At God's own choosing, He also may call His child home because of the sin of **omission** (*as with disobedient prophet of I Kings 13:21-22*).

> *James 4:17: Therefore to him that knoweth to do good, and doeth it not, to him it is sin.*

For some, a reluctance to serve God and witness of His grace may be a sin of omission, and may be the cause of a sin unto death.

How Does a Man Sin?

> *James 1:14-16: But every man is tempted (solicited to evil) when he is drawn away* **of his own lust***, and enticed. Then when lust hath conceived, it bringeth forth sin: and sin, when it is finished, bringeth forth death. Do not err, my* **beloved brethren***.*

74

The children of God (*beloved brethren*) in this context are admonished, that ye **sin not**, and if believers sin, they have an advocate with the Father" (*I John 2:2*). Confession and forsaking of sin is required.

> *I John 1:8: If we say that we have **no sin**, **we** (believers) **deceive ourselves**, and the truth is not in us.*

Obviously, John is not talking to unbelievers here because the unsaved are condemned already and living in sin (*John 3:18, 36*), and are also referred to as sinners.

When referring to his flesh, the apostle Paul plainly stated, sin dwelleth in me

(*Romans 7:17-25*). Paul is contrasting the **flesh** (*the old man of Ephesians 4:22*) to the inward, **spiritual man** (*the new man of Ephesians 4:24*). The believer has **two natures,** the divine (*Christ in you*) and the adamic (*fleshly nature of Adam*). The unbeliever has only one nature, the sinful flesh, which was inherited from his father, who inherited it from his father who inherited it right on down the family line to the genealogical family father of all, Adam.

The Children of God are warned about the weakness of the flesh.

> *Matthew 26:41: Watch and pray, that ye enter not into temptation: the **spirit** indeed is willing, but the **flesh** is weak.*

> *Galatians 5:17: For the **flesh** lusteth against the Spirit, and the **Spirit** against the flesh: and these are contrary the one to the other: so that ye cannot do the things that ye would.*

Paul details fuller the **adamic nature** of a believer in Romans 7:15-25.

If our Arminian brethren believe in the two natures of the believer, why are many of them **silen**t about teaching or preaching on it. A believer can and does sin through the weakness of the flesh. As stated previously, God **will** allow His own children to fall into sin, but He **will not** allow them to continually lie in it. Even the chastening of the Lord is the peaceable assurance of salvation (*Hebrews 12:6-11*).

Willful Presumptuous Sin

To sin willfully (*deliberately*) after receiving the knowledge of the truth would leave no more sacrifice for sin.

> *Hebrews 10:26: For if we sin **wilfully** after that we have received the knowledge of the truth, there remaineth **no more sacrifice for sin**.*

This text in Hebrews applies to legalistic Jews who had mentally accepted Christ as a prophet of God, but many had NOT put their faith in Christ as their promised Messiah. Legalistic Jews were still clinging to Mosaic law-keeping instead of trusting in Jesus as their sacrifice for sin. They had **come near** to God's grace but presumptuously sinned after receiving the knowledge of the truth. These legalists were told that there remained no more sacrifice for their sin (*Hebrews 10:26*), if they refused the ONLY true sacrifice.

God's sacrifice was *"...the **Lamb of God**, which taketh away the sin of the world."* The Lord Jesus Christ **was,** and **is** the **only** sacrifice that justifies man's salvation (*John 1:29*).

Hebrews 10:26 is not a case of a saved person becoming lost and then returning to seek a sacrifice for their sin. Even **if** (*hypothetically, but not possible*) a believer could become lost again, he could not return again to the Lord for repentance for there remained **no more sacrifice** for his *presumptuous* sin.

76

The Believer's Sin (Past-Present-Future)

The sin of a saint does not change his **standing** (*salvation*), but his sin does terminate his **state** (*fellowship*) with the Lord. Again, Jesus paid the price for ALL of the believer's sin, not for **past** sin only. There is an erroneous assumption among many brethren that only the past sins of saints are forgiven. It is very probable, that genuine believers, daily, commit sins of commission, sins of omission, sins of laziness, sins of ignorance, sins of prayerlessness, and sins of failing to love their neighbor as themselves. However, God is faithful and merciful to His saints and has removed their transgressions from them.

Forgiveness Of Sin Is Forever

Psalms 103:12: As far as the east is from the west, so far hath He removed our transgressions from us.

(The north and south poles have endings. There are no endings of the east and west.)

*Hebrews 8:12: For I will be merciful to their unrighteousness, and their **sins and their iniquities will I remember no more.***

*Hebrews 7:25: Wherefore He is able also to save them to the uttermost (completely)that come unto God by Him, seeing **He ever liveth to make intercession for them**.*

*Isaiah 38:17: "...for Thou hast cast **all** my sins behind Thy back."*

*Isaiah 44:22: I have **blotted out**, as a thick cloud, **thy transgressions**, and, as a cloud, **thy sins**: return unto Me; for **I have redeemed thee**.*

*Micah 7:19: He will turn again, He will have compassion upon us; **He will subdue our iniquities**; and Thou wilt cast **all** their sins into the depths of the sea.*

(Again, it is nowhere implied that only past sins are forgiven.)

> *Jeremiah 31:34: And they shall teach no more every man his neighbour, and every man his brother, saying, Know the LORD: for they all shall know Me, from the least of them unto the greatest of them, saith the LORD: for I will forgive their iniquity,* **and I will remember their sin no more.**

Although the verse in Jeremiah 31:34 concerns Israel and Judah, it can also be applied to individual Jews and includes Gentile believers graffed (*grafted*) into the New Covenant of Grace (*Jeremiah 31:31-34; Romans 11:24*).Israel and Judah had broken the Old Covenant by idolatry (*spiritual adultery*). By the finger of God, His Spirit of New Covenant Grace is written upon the hearts of New Testament believers (*Jeremiah 31:32*).

The Believer's Chastening and the Sin Unto Death

It bears being repeated many times over, God chastens ALL of His children. **Sinning** saints will be chastened of the Lord (*Hebrews 12:5-8*), and if they do not respond to God's chastening hand, they may forfeit their physical lives prematurely (*sin unto death*); however, they will be saved (*I Corinthians 3:15; 5:5*).Unsaved church members (*children of the devil - John 8:44*) will be judged and cast into the lake of fire (*Matthew 7:15; 13:19-22; 22:12-14; 23:28; Revelation 20:11-15*).

Afflictions of the flesh and harsh trials of the believer are not all because of sin; God uses various trials to test our faith and cause us to grow in grace.

The Book of Hebrews explicitly states that **God chastens every son** whom He receives:

*Hebrews 12:5-8: And ye have forgotten the exhortation which speaketh unto you as unto children, **My son**, despise not thou the **chastening** of the Lord, nor faint when thou art rebuked of Him: For whom the Lord loveth **He chasteneth and scourgeth every son whom He receiveth**. If ye endure **chastening**, God dealeth with you as with sons; for what son is he whom the father chasteneth not? **But if ye be without chastisement**, whereof **all** are partakers, **then are ye bastards, and not sons.***

A son that sins will be chastened of the Lord. If there is no chastening, the person is a bastard (illegitimate), not a son. Again, if the chastening of the Lord is not heeded, the unrepentant son may commit a sin unto death, forfeiting his life **prematurely**.

*I John 5:16-17: If any man see **his brother** sin a sin which is not unto death, he shall ask, and he shall give him life for them that sin not unto death. **There is a sin unto death**. I do not say that he shall pray for it. All unrighteousness is sin: and **there is a sin not unto death**.*

*Romans 6:16: Know ye not, that to whom ye yield yourselves servants to obey, his servants ye are to whom ye obey; whether of **sin unto death**, or of obedience unto righteousness?*

God chastens the sinning saint that he should not be condemned with the lost world.

*I Corinthians 11:32: But when we are judged we are **chastened** of the Lord, that we should **not be condemned** with the world.*

A sinning believer of the Bible:

The unrepentant sinning saint of I Corinthians 5:1-5 was to be delivered unto Satan for the destruction of the flesh that the spirit may be saved in the day of the

Lord Jesus. He had been guilty of the incestuous act of fornication with his father's wife (step-mother).

The writer believes that he has seen several instances of believers whose lives have been cut short by committing a sin unto death. Although this writer may be wrong about some of these incidents, he is not wrong concerning the Scriptural teaching itself of a believer committing a sin unto death. Even Moses and Aaron, chosen of God, met an untimely death.

Abusing the Lord's Supper:

A believer may die prematurely by observing the Lord's Supper in an unworthy manner.

> *I Corinthians 11:30: For this cause many are weak and sickly among you, and many **sleep** (die). See I Corinthians 11:18-32.*

In the Old Testament, King David's *physical* life was spared because he had confessed and repented of his sin (*Psalms 51:3*):

> *2 Samuel 12:13: And David said unto Nathan, **I have sinned** against the LORD. And Nathan said unto David, The LORD also hath put away thy sin; **thou shalt not die**.*

When the prophet Nathan confronted David (*using a parable of one little ewe lamb*) concerning his sin in the matter of Uriah, David repented and unknowingly prophesied his own particular judgment as **four-fold** (*2 Samuel 12:6*).

Ironically, David's children would be his **four-fold** grief:

1. **death** of his child (by the adulterous affair with Bathsheba)

2. **rape** of his virgin daughter, Tamar, by her half-brother, Amnon

80

3. vengeful **murder** of Amnon by Tamar's brother, Absalom

4. **treason** and death of Absalom, David's son

David's sons, Absalom, Amnon, and Adonijah all fell by the sword. David was to be chastened of the Lord all of his days (*The sword shall not depart from thine house – Second Samuel 12:10*), but David was not condemned to Hell with the world.

Works Do Not Justify

In the book of Corinthians, we see that a man's **work may be burned** and he shall **suffer loss of rewards,** but **he himself shall be saved** yet so as by fire.

> *I Corinthians 3:14-15: If any man's **work** abide which he hath built thereupon, he shall receive a **reward**.If any man's **work** shall be burned, he shall suffer loss: **but he himself shall be saved**; yet so as by fire.*

It is doubtful that Lot, Abraham's nephew, had any good works; he chose to live among the abominable Sodomites, but even so, he was a saved man. Lot's soul was vexed with the filthy habitation of the wicked (*Genesis 13:12; 19:1; Luke 17:28-29*). However, Lot was accounted as just.

> *2 Peter 2:7: And delivered **just Lot** vexed with the filthy conversation of the wicked.*

Presumptuous Sins of Bible Heroes

- **Abraham** had concubines, and presumptuously lied about Sarah his wife, twice. If God has not intervened, Pharaoh (*Genesis 12:15*) and Abimelech (*Genesis 20:2*) would have defiled Sarah in bed.

81

- **Isaac** presumptuously lied about Rebekah, his wife (*Genesis 26:7*). He thought to save his skin as his father Abraham had done.

- **Jacob** had multiple wives (*polygamy*) and handmaids (*secondary wives*) - Genesis 35:23-26. (***Not** to their praise, many of the OT patriarchs had multiple wives*).

- -Adam peopled the world with one wife; Noah peopled the world with one wife!

- **David,** one of God's greatest men, presumptuously sinned: he committed polygamy (*I Samuel 25:42; 2 Samuel 3:2-5; 5:13-15*); adultery (*2 Samuel 11:3, 4*); murder (2 Samuel 11:15; I King 15:5). In his pride, he also sinned in the matter of numbering Israel (*2 Samuel 24:10*).

- **Solomon,** known for his great wisdom, presumptuously sinned by sacrificing in high places, and unwisely loved many strange women (700 wives and princesses [*polygamy*], plus 300 concubines - *I Kings 11:3*).

- **Samson** presumptuously sinned by laying with harlots (*Judges 16:1, 4*).

- **Peter** sinned presumptuously by his thrice denial of Christ; he also cursed and swore (*Matthew 26:73*).

Believers can fall into sin and many do; but they do not get by with it. God promises that every sinning saint will be chastened. The believer's failure to repent and forsake his sin may end as a sin unto death (*Romans 6:16; I John 5:16*). This sin unto death of the believer is **not** an unpardonable sin. Neither is it the blasphemy against the Holy Ghost. The sin unto death, is, in context, **a sin committed by a Christian brother,** as expressed in I John 5:16 "If any man see **his brother** sin a sin...There is a sin unto death..." A Christian can persist in some known sin, though not the sin of total unbelief or willful apostasy, because a true Christian will not commit that kind of sin. If the Christian deliberately continues to practice ungodliness in doctrine or his daily living and does not respond to God's chastening, the Lord may require his life; however, the sinning Christian will not suffer eternal death, "He shall **suffer loss**: but he himself **shall be saved**..." (*I Corinthians 3:15*). God **will** allow his children to sin but He **will not** allow them to habitually live in it.

I Corinthians 11:30-32: For this cause (*partaking of the Lord's Supper unworthily*) many *are* weak and sickly among you, and many **sleep (***die***)**. For if we would judge ourselves, we should not be judged. But when we are judged we are chastened of the Lord, **that we should not be condemned with the world**.

It is also evident in the Scriptures that the unsaved (*as well as the saved*) also commit sins unto death (*Genesis 38:7, 10; I Chronicles 2:3; I Samuel 2:25*). In the NT, it certainly appears that King Herod did so, as indicated by Jesus' refusal to answer Herod's inquiry.

Luke 23:9: Then he (Herod) questioned with him in many words; but He (Jesus) answered him nothing.

For the Believer, Sin is in a Three-Fold Tense of Past, Present, and Future

Three-Fold Tense	Saved From	Theology	Jesus' Role
1. We were saved	Past Penalty of sin	Justification	Prophet
2. We are saved	Present Power of Sin	Sanctification	Priest
3. We will be saved	Presence of sin	Glorification	King

Some Christians think of salvation merely as having one's sins forgiven, but salvation is only the beginning of the new man in Christ. The OT believer under Mosaic Law was required annually to present the body and blood of an innocent animal as a dead sacrifice to cover his sin (*until the perfect Sacrifice of Jesus would be offered*). The NT believer is to present his own body as a living sacrifice of praise, worship, and service.

Two Influences of the Will

The free will of all men to exercise faith in Christ for salvation is denied by our Hyper-Calvinist brethren. At the other end of the theological spectrum, our Arminian brethren suppose that because a man possesses a free will, he can, and will at any time reject Christ after having received Him. It must be understood that man will never operate apart from both **inside** and **outside** influences. Scriptures state that the **unsaved** have their wills under the influence and dominion of the prince of the power of the air, the spirit that now worketh in the children of disobedience (*Ephesians 2:2, 9; 2 Cor. 4:4; 2 Tim. 2:26*).In opposition to the satanic influence upon the unsaved, the Scriptures state that the will of the **saved** person is under the power and influence of the Spirit of God, the Word of God plainly states that it is God which worketh in you, both to will and to do of His good pleasure (*Philippians 2:13*). God will not suffer His saints to be tempted above that they are able to bear (*I Corinthians 10:13*).

No one can deny that the Scriptures teach that God is able to save, and that He is able to keep the saved one from falling (*Romans 14:4; 2 Timothy 1:12; Jude 4; Hebrews 7:25; I Peter 1:5; Psalm 121:5*). The important question is: Will God? Will God, who is able to keep His child from being lost, exercise that power and actually keep him, or will God desert him and permit Satan alone to influence his will? There are many Scriptures that give

84

God's assurance of the believer's security in his salvation. The book of Romans gives explicit assurance of God's protective care.

> *Romans 5:8-10: But God commendeth His love toward us, in that, while we were yet sinners, Christ died for us.* **Much more then**, *being now justified by His blood, we shall be* **saved from wrath** *through Him. For if, when we were enemies we were reconciled to God by the death of His Son,* **Much more**, *being reconciled we shall be* **saved by His life**.

> *Christ ever* **liveth** *to make intercession for us (Hebrews 7:25).*

If God will save a sinner upon the basis **of the death** of Christ, He will **MUCH MORE** keep the saint from the wrath to come **by the life** of Christ's, ministry, **intercession** and resurrection power.

(**Intercession:** The believer's security falls under the head of Christ's intercessory work at the right hand of God. Christ's intercession has nothing to do with the unsaved; it is only for those whom God has given Christ – *John 17:11-12, 20, 24; Hebrews 7:25*.)

> *I Peter 1:5: Who are* **kept by the power of God** *through faith unto salvation ready to be revealed in the last time.*

> *Psalms 121:5:* **The LORD is thy Keeper**: *the LORD is thy shade upon thy right hand.*

> *Hebrews 13:5: Let your conversation be without covetousness; and be content with such things as ye have: for He hath said, I will* **never leave thee, nor forsake thee**.

It does not follow that you can reject Christ after having received Him.

John 6:37: ***All*** *that the Father giveth Me shall come to Me; and him that cometh to Me* ***I will in no wise cast out****.*

A Saint Can Both Sin and Not Sin

I John 1:7: *If we* (believers) *say that we have no sin, we deceive ourselves, and the truth is not in us.*

This message is to believers, not to the unsaved (*I John 2:1*); it is evident that unbelievers are outside the kingdom of God and are practicing sinners. Even the most godly Christian may sin occasionally, either in thought if not in deed, or in omission if not in commission (*I John 1:8, 10; Matthew 5:28; Romans 3:10, 12; 5:8, 12; Galatians 3:3; James 4:17; Isaiah 64:6*).If a Christian could live an immaculate life to the absolute point of perfection, in body, soul, and spirit, he would be without sin. There are no such people and neither has there ever been. No one has ever been able to be justified by perfectly keeping the commandments of God (Except of course, Christ the God-man).However, there is a danger if we use Scriptures to prove our inability to keep the whole Law of God perfectly. There is no excuse for sinning or even taking sin too lightly.

Christ Imputes His Righteousness To His Saints

I John 3:9: Whosoever is born of God ***doth not commit sin****; for His seed remaineth in him: and he cannot sin, because he is born of God.*

Of course, here is meant of the divine life of the new nature of the Holy Spirit, who indwells believers at the very time of salvation (*2 Peter 1:4*). Saints are born of God, and they are in Christ, and His righteousness has been imputed them that believe. The believer's sin has been charged to and paid for by Jesus Christ. The Spirit of God indwells ALL believers (*Romans 8:9; John 14:16, 17;*

86

16:7, 13). If we are in Christ and He (Christ) cannot sin, neither can we. Our sins have been put upon Christ who cannot sin. Neither can the believer live or practice a lifestyle of sin and rebellion. God has commanded us not to sin and He would not command us to do the impossible. For every temptation, there is a way to escape (*I Corinthians 10:13*). In Christ, every provision necessary to **not** sin has been provided by God. We are without any legitimate excuse whenever we willingly sin. However, this cannot be misconstrued to mean that Christians *never* sin in the flesh (*I John 1:8, 10*). Temptation itself is not sin; it is the entertaining and yielding to the temptation that becomes sin. Actually, sin alone is not the final ruin of man; it is man's failure to repent (*Luke 13:3, 5)* and believe the Gospel (*John 3:16*). For ALL have sinned (*Romans 3:23; I John 1:8, 10*).

Beware of private interpretations, philosophies, dogmas, and unorthodox traditions of men - *Matthew 15:3; Mark 7:13; Colossians 2:8; I Peter 1:18; II Peter 1:20*).

Nothing Can Separate a Believer From the Love of Christ

Romans 8:35-39: **Who shall separate us from the love of Christ?** *shall* **tribulation**, *or* **distress**, *or* **persecution**, *or* **famine**, *or* **nakedness**, *or peril, or* **sword**? *As it is written, For Thy sake we are killed all the day long; we are accounted as sheep for the slaughter. Nay, in all these things we are more than conquerors through Him that loved us. For I am persuaded, that neither* **death**, *nor* **life**, *nor* **angels**, *nor* **principalities**, *nor* **powers**, *nor* **things present**, *nor* **things to come**, *Nor* **height**, *nor* **depth**, *nor* **any other creature**, *shall be able to separate us from the love of God which is in Christ Jesus our Lord.*

87

If nothing less than God's Son could save us, then nothing less could lose us.

The things listed in Romans 8:35-39 cover everything except God Himself. Can the reader think of any other thing that is not covered in this text? Neither can God separate us for He has promised that He would never leave us nor forsake us (*Hebrews 13:5; John 6:37*). Neither can God break His promise of the gift of eternal life because the Scriptures cannot be broken (*John 10:35*); Neither can God lie (*Titus 1:2; Hebrews 6:18*).

The Sheep of Jesus Will Never Perish

John 10:26-29: But ye believe not, because ye are not of My sheep, as I said unto you. My Sheep hear My voice, and I know them, and they follow Me: And I give unto them eternal life; and they shall never perish, neither shall any man pluck them out of My hand. My Father, which gave them Me, is greater than all; and no man is able to pluck them out of My Father's hand.

Jesus' sheep shall **never perish** because Jesus **gives** them eternal life. Notice that Jesus did not say that He will give (*future tense*) His sheep eternal life at some future time. The gift of eternal life is a present possession for His sheep. Salvation of a saint is 100 % unconditional; the security of the believer's salvation is not based upon any degree of the saint's own virtue to either obtain or retain it. The verb, give, used of Jesus is in the present tense and implies future continuance. Salvation is a permanent gift (*eternal life*) and John tells us (*John 10:26-29)* that no **power** is able to pluck His sheep from the hands of the Father and Son.

(Note: The word *man* is *italicized* in both verses of John 10:28-29 in the King James Bible. This italicization indicates that the word *man* was not in the Greek manuscript but was supplied by the translators for clarity;

consequently, the text without the word man, implies *force* or *power,* whether of man or any other entity.)

Not only are believers secure in the hands of the Father and the Son, but they are also sealed by the Holy Spirit of promise (*Ephesians 1:13; 4:30; 2 Corinthians 1:22*). The writer thinks that this is assurance of the Great trinitarian Three-In-One God.

The Shepherd's Care of His Sheep

The **23rd Psalm**, probably the best-loved chapter in the Bible, finds it exposition in the **10th chapter of John**. Christ is the Good Shepherd who gives His life for the sheep (*John 10:11*). The **6 verses** of Psalm 23 each contain a different testimony concerning the Shepherd's protective care of His sheep (*They shall never perish - John 10:28*). Corresponding numerically, the word shepherd is used **6 times** in John 10 (*vv. 2, 11 twice, 12, 14, 16*). Christ is also referred to as shepherd in **6 other NT books.**

In Psalm 23, David uses the first person pronouns ("I, Me, My," etc.) **17 times** in its **6 verses**. When the Day of Pentecost was fully come, there were dwelling at Jerusalem about **17** groups of Jews of every nation (*Acts 2:1-11*). The word, sheep, is used **17 times** in John 10. The 8th chapter of Romans lists about **17 things** that can never separate believers from the love of Christ (*Romans 8:35-39*). Noah's Ark rested on the 17th day of the month (*Genesis 8:4*), perhaps suggesting that judgment was past. Christ arose from the grave on the 17th day of the month. If Christ lives, we shall live also and judgment is past.

E.W. Bullinger (*Numbers in Scripture*, Kregel Publications) reckons the **number 17** to mean, the perfection of spiritual order. Of course, numbers may not be relied upon for teaching Bible doctrine, but their numerical significance can be a blessing.

This writer thinks that Psalms chapter 23, John chapter 10, and Romans chapter 8 are probably three of the greatest chapters in the Bible that clearly expresses the believer's security.

Psalms 23 closes with "...and **I will** dwell in the house of the LORD for ever." It is not, I might or I may, dwell in the house of the Lord if I am faithful enough, strong enough, or spiritual enough to get to Heaven, but the presumptuous, I will.

Of course, some of our Arminian brethren would erroneously assert that the presumptuous, I will, is only applicable in a futuristic sense of believers that are already in Heaven.

Salvation is a Present Reality

John 3:15: That whosoever believeth in Him **should not perish**, *but* **have** *eternal life.*

Again, notice the **present tense** of the verb, have (Greek, *echo*), which says that **presently, right now,** we have eternal life (*not contingent upon anything of our own doing*). In the matter of salvation, **all** of our sins (*past; present; future*) have been paid for by the sacrificial death of Christ, and will be remembered against us no more. **If (***but not possible***)** man could assist his salvation in the smallest degree, there would be many braggarts in Heaven.

Though we seldom use it, we have the capacity to think God's thoughts after Him.

I Corinthians 2:16: For who hath known the mind of the Lord, that he may instruct him? **But we have the mind of Christ**.

John 10:27-28: And I **give** *unto them eternal life; and they shall* **never perish**, *neither shall any man (power; entity; mechanism) pluck them out of My hand*

90

Eternal Life is Fully Contingent Upon God

If eternal life (salvation) could be interrupted **anywhere** in the process of time, eternal life could not be expressed as eternal. It is not eternal life if it is dependent upon believers to hold out or retain their integrity toward God. Eternal life of the saints begins at the moment of salvation and is without end. Our Arminian brethren believe that God's saints are **preserved in Heaven**, but they do not believe that they are **preserved upon earth**. The Psalmist believed that the LORD would **keep** His people during life (*on earth*) and after death (*in Heaven*):

> *Psalms 121:7-8: The LORD shall **preserve** thee from all evil: He shall **preserve thy soul**. The LORD shall **preserve** thy going out and thy coming in **from this time forth, and even for evermore**.*

> *Jude 1:1: Jude, the servant of Jesus Christ, and brother of James, to them that are sanctified by God the Father, and **preserved** in Jesus Christ, and called.*

Preserved speaks of eternal life and the security of the believer.

Psalms 121:5 expressly states, The LORD is **thy keeper.** Our Arminian brethren say that we are our own keeper and we can choose to remove ourselves from the hand of God. What crazy person in the world would deliberately seek to pluck himself out of God's hand (*If it were possible*) and choose Hell over Heaven? Of course, our Arminian brethren claim that God will forsake you if you sin. Does the reader know of any saint that does not sin to some degree and in some fashion? There is no such thing as a Christian who does not sin in the flesh(*I John 1:8, 10; Romans 3:10, 23; 7:17, 18, 25; Isaiah 53:6; 64:6*). Of course, fellowship is broken by sin. Our **standing** (salvation*)* is secure even when our **state**

91

(fellowship) is not. God **will** depart His fellowship from a sinning believer. The **union** is secure if the **unity** is not. There is no sin temptation that can overcome a saint's salvation and remove him from God's hand. As for God forsaking the believer, that question was answered before. He promised to **never** leave us (believers) nor forsake us (*Deuteronomy 31:6; Hebrews 13:5; John 6:37*). God cannot lie (*Titus 1:2; Hebrews 6:18*).

> *Hebrews 13:5:* "...for He hath said, I will never leave thee, nor forsake thee."

The Bible scholar, Henry M. Morris, says, "Hebrews 13:5 has five negatives in the Greek and could be rendered literally as something like, *I will **never, never** leave thee, and **never, never, never** forsake thee.*"

Eternal life (salvation) is everlasting because it is in **the blood of the Everlasting Covenant** (*Hebrews 13:20*).

> *I Corinthians 10:13: There hath **no temptation** taken you but such as is common to man: but God is faithful, **Who will not suffer you to be tempted above that ye are able**; but will with the temptation also make a way to escape, that ye may be able to bear it.*

> *Psalms 37:24: Though he fall, he shall not be utterly* (completely) *cast down: for **the LORD upholdeth him with His hand.***

A believer may fall IN salvation, but he does not fall OUT of salvation.

Jesus is the only man (God-man) whoever lived and is alive for evermore (*Revelation 1:18*) **who is without sin** (*John 8:46; 2 Corinthians 5:21; Hebrews 4:15; James 1:13*).Jesus took the believer's sin upon Himself on the cross of Calvary and imputed His righteousness to believers by grace through faith (*Ephesians 2:8-9*).

92

When a Christian sins, he **loses fellowship** and **loses rewards** (*I Corinthians 3:12-15; 2 John 8*), but he does not lose his soul. The **believer's sin was settled and paid for in full at Calvary**. **All of the believers' sins** (*past, present, and future*) were put upon Jesus. Jesus bore it **all**.

Are Backsliders Lost?

In Christendom (*the sphere of Christian profession*), losing fellowship (*not salvation*) with God is commonly referred to as, backsliding. However, Christians have different opinions of the meaning of backsliding. Some believe that backsliders go to Hell if not repentant.

Question # 1: If (*hypothetically*) the backslider is lost, why would he refuse to repent knowing that all earthly things are come to an end and only Hell awaited him? Only an absolute idiot would refuse to repent. Of course, any backslid Christian would repent!

Question # 2: If (*hypothetically*) backsliders are former saved people that became lost, and afterwards return again in repentance and faith, do they get born again a second or third time? Please give a verse or text that supports multiple salvations for the same person!

Actually, the word, backslider, is not in the New Testament Scriptures at all. The three forms of backslider (*backslider; backsliding; backslidings*) occur **17 times** in three books of the Old Testament, *Proverbs, Jeremiah, and Hosea*. Backslider is primarily a corporate term referring to the 10 Northern Tribes of Israel that revolted under Jeroboam's leadership. Israel withdrew from Judah after Solomon's death and its new leader, Jeroboam, introduced idolatry into the 10 Northern Tribes. It grieved God that Israel committed spiritual adultery as did her treacherous sister, Judah (*Jeremiah 3:6-8, 11-13, 22; 8:5; 49:4; Hosea 4:16; 11:7; 14:4; Proverbs 14:14*).

However, the Lord was a husband unto backsliding Israel (*Jeremiah 31:22*).

Both Israel and Judah were punished, but God's Covenant with them was not broken. God told them to acknowledge their iniquity and turn, "...**for I am married unto you**" (*Jeremiah 3:14*).

Even though Israel was bent to backsliding, God does not give her up:

> *Hosea 11:7-9: "And My people are bent to backsliding from Me: how shall I give thee up, Ephraim (10 Northern Tribes of Israel)? how shall I deliver thee, Israel?...I will not execute the fierceness of Mine anger, I will not return to destroy Ephraim: for I am God, and not man..."*

Israel has **not** been cast away forever regardless of her backsliding (*Romans 11:1-2; Psalms 94:14*). Blindness in part is happened to Israel **until** the fullness of the Gentiles be come in (*Romans 11:25*). God has given Israel the spirit of slumber (*Romans 11:8*). And so all Israel (corporate; *the nation*) shall be saved (*Romans 11:26*).

Although adulterous Israel has been set aside for a time because of her backsliding ways, she is the **wife of Jehovah** and not destined to be forever abandoned. The backslider in heart shall be filled with his own ways (*Proverbs 14:14*). Neither Israel's backslidings nor the loss of fellowship relate to the loss of a believer's salvation.

In his book, *Bible Questions Answered,* William Pettingill states, "No matter how backslidden a child of God may be, he never boasts of his backsliding, nor claims the right to backslide. He remains a child of God all the time, and he is wretched, even while living in disobedience of God's Word and will."

Believers Are Redeemed Already; The Body Awaits Redemption

Romans 8:23: And not only they, but ourselves also, which have the firstfruits of the Spirit, even we ourselves groan within ourselves, **waiting for the adoption, to wit, the redemption of our body.** *(See also 2 Corinthians 4:16; Ephesians 3:16; 4:22.).*

The saved were chosen in Christ before the foundation of the world (*Ephesians 1:4*). God knew in the beginning (*omniscience; foreknowledge*) those who would believe and decreed beforehand that they would be chosen to salvation (the elect) and ultimately be like unto Christ (in the resurrection). If any are lost, God's choice failed and God's eternal plan and purpose would be disrupted.

It is easy to suppose that a man is saved because he reforms, or becomes religious and appears to live a Christian life. If there are false apostles, why should Christians be surprised at unsaved church members simulating the lifestyle of true believers? Satan himself is transformed into an angel of light and his ministers as ministers of righteousness (*2 Corinthians 11:13-15*),

Can a Person Live Holy Enough to Be Assured of Heaven?

If (*hypothetically, but not possible*) any person could obtain Heaven by his own merit, he would have to keep the whole body of law perfectly as Jesus did upon earth. Surely Heaven would be full of the prideful, **if** man could obtain (*or retain*) salvation by his own efforts. **If** it were possible for man to be saved by living an absolute holy life (as Christ lived), it would **not** have been necessary for Jesus to have condescended to the form of a man and endure great pain, humiliation and shame,

95

upon a cruel Roman cross. Jesus kept the law perfectly in the believer's stead and good works outweighing bad works count for nothing (*nought, nada, nil*).

> *James 2:10: For whosoever shall keep the whole law, and yet offend in one point, he is guilty of all.* (See also Galatians 2:21; 3:10, 13; 5:3; Romans 10:5.)

Believers are Kept and Sealed by The Power of God

It is of no significance of what men may say or how men may feel about the security of believers. The all-important fact is, **What doth the Scriptures say?**

Psalms 121:5 says,

> *"The LORD is thy **Keeper**: the LORD is thy Shade upon thy right hand."*

> *I Peter 1:5: Who* (saints) *are **kept by the power of God** through faith unto salvation ready to be revealed in the last time.*

> *Ephesians 4:30: And grieve not the Holy Spirit of God, whereby **ye** (all) **are sealed** unto the day of redemption* (of the body; the soul and spirit are already redeemed).

The sealed work of the Spirit is a finished work (conclusive; final) and it cannot be unsealed or broken, even though the believer may grieve the Holy Spirit with sin.

> *2 Corinthians 1:22: Who hath also **sealed us**, and given **the earnest of the Spirit** in our hearts.*

The earnest of the Spirit (*2 Corinthians 5:5),* is the pledge that secures the full payment. Many attempt to explain away these plainly stated Scriptures, but instead, reveal the lack of their assurance of salvation. Some like to add that it is the salvation itself that is sealed, but not the believer (?). The soul is redeemed already (*Romans 8:23*).

Paul said,

*"...for I know whom I have believed, and am persuaded that **he is able to keep that which I have committed unto Him** against that day" (II Timothy 1:12).*

Obviously, Paul was **not** talking about committing his earthly flesh (*"They that are in the flesh cannot please God"* - *Romans 8:8*); Paul was speaking primarily of committing his spirit and soul (*and also his future redeemed body*). Is there any other safer haven for the soul than committing it unto the Lord? Of course not! Our Arminian brethren **add to** this verse. They say that God is able to keep you, but He may not.

The prayer of Jesus was for the Father to KEEP His saints:

*John 17:11: And now I am no more in the world, but these are in the world, and I come to Thee. Holy Father, **keep** them through Thine own name those whom Thou has given Me, that they may be one, as We are.*

Does the reader doubt that Jesus' prayer was answered? **None** are lost (*John 17:12*).

The Preacher of Ecclesiastes Believed that God's Works Were Forever:

*Ecclesiastes 3:14: I know that, **whatsoever God doeth, it shall be for ever**: nothing **can be put to it, nor any thing taken from it**: and God doeth it, that men should fear before Him.*

Whatsoever God doeth, includes the salvation of a soul as well as the condemnation of the soul. When God saves a soul, it is **forever** and nothing can be taken from it because **God doeth it**.

97

The Good Work of Salvation Is **Begun** by God and also **Maintained** by Him:

> *Philippians 1:6: Being confident of this very thing,* **that He which hath begun a good work in you will perform it** *until the day of Jesus Christ.*

> *Philippians 2:13: For it is God which* **worketh in you** *both to will and to do of His good pleasure.*

Believers at the Church of Corinth

The apostle Paul assured the carnal believers of the church of Corinth that they would be blameless in the day of our Lord Jesus Christ:

> *I Corinthians 1:8: Who shall also* **confirm you unto the end**, *that ye may be blameless in the day of our Lord Jesus Christ.*

Carnal believers of the Corinth Church were Confirmed Unto the End. Their salvation was secure in spite of their guiltiness in mattes of the carnal nature. These carnal believers were guilty of: divisions (*I Cor. 1:10; 3:3; 11:18*); contentions (*I Cor. 1:11*); glorying (*I Cor. 1:31: 5:6*); carnality (*I Cor. 3:1, 3, 4*); envying (*I Cor. 3:3*); strife (*I Cor. 3:3*); being puffed up (*I Cor. 4:18, 19: 5:2*); fornication (*I Cor. 5:1*); bad company (*I Cor. 5:9-11*); going to the law (*I Cor. 6:1, 7*); defrauding one another (*I Cor. 6:8*); heresies (*I Cor. 11:19*); drunkenness (*I Cor. 11:21*); walking as men (*I Cor. 3:3*). The list continues on: debates, envyings, wraths, strifes, backbitings, whisperings, swellings, tumults, uncleanness, fornication, and lasciviousness (*2 Cor. 12:20-21*). If these carnal believers were secure in salvation, who are the sinning believers that will not be confirmed unto the end? David, a man after God's own heart, committed adultery and murder, yet David was saved in the end. If he had **not** repented of his sin, his earthly life would have been forfeited prematurely (*2 Samuel 12:13*), but his spirit would have been saved just as the carnal believers of Corinth.

> *I Corinthians 5:5: To deliver such an one unto Satan for the destruction of the flesh, **that the spirit may be saved** in the day of the Lord Jesus.*

Although man is unable to live holy enough to merit Heaven, a saved person is able to live a holy, sanctified, Spirit-filled life, apart from committing sin. Nowhere in Scriptures is a sinning religion (*antinomianism*) justified. If a professing believer can continue to practice a sinful lifestyle without experiencing conviction and chastisement, his faith is questionable.

In reference to Paul's writings, Peter says,

> *"...in which are **some things hard to be understood**, which **they that are unlearned and unstable wrest**, as they do also the other Scriptures, unto their own destruction"* (2 Peter 3:16).

> *Matthew 7:22-23: **Many** will say to Me in that day, Lord, Lord, have we not **prophesied in Thy name:** and in Thy name have **cast out devils**? and in Thy name **done many wonderful works**? And then will I profess unto them, **I never knew you**: depart from Me, ye that work iniquity.*

> *Matthew 23:27-28: Woe unto you, scribes and Pharisees, hypocrites! For ye are like unto whited sepulchres, which indeed appear beautiful **outward**, but are within full of dead men's bones, and of all uncleanness. Even so ye also **outwardly appear righteous unto men**, but within ye are full of hypocrisy and iniquity.*

> *Proverbs 14:12; 16:25: There is **a way that seemeth right** unto a man, but the end thereof are **the ways of death**.*

99

According to the above Scriptures, **unsaved** religious people will be horribly shocked after death when they face God only to hear that they are lost forever. Conversely, many **saved** people **without full assurance** of their salvation will awaken, and to their surprise, discover that they really are saved (*Hebrews 6:11*). Those that were erroneously depending upon their own efforts to retain eternal life thought it too presumptuous to accept God's **promise of eternal life**.

> *Hebrews 7:25: Wherefore He is able* (Jude 24) *also to save them to the uttermost* (completely) *that come unto God by Him, seeing that He* (Jesus) *ever liveth to make intercession for them.*

Only ONE Salvation

> *Hebrews 6:4-6: For* ***it is impossible*** *for those who were once enlightened, and have tasted of the heavenly gift, and were made partakers of the Holy Ghost, And have tasted the good word of God, and the powers of the world to come,* ***If*** *they shall fall away, to renew them again unto repentance; seeing* ***they crucify to themselves the Son of God afresh****, and put Him to an open shame*

Again, **if** (*hypothetically*) this passage teaches the *possibility* of one losing salvation, it also teaches the *impossibility* of regaining it. Of course, the passage is not teaching that a saved person can become lost again; it does, very clearly, state that they cannot return to crucify Christ anew. Actually, the passage is, in context, in reference to **Israelites at Kadesh-barnea,** which is alluded to in Hebrews chapters three and four. Israel had provoked Jehovah which foreshadowed the crisis confronting the Hebrew nation of entering into the promised land. Israel had been enlightened (*Numbers 14*), tasted of the fruits of Canaan, experienced miraculous powers, and tasted the good Word of God but had turned back in unbelief. Applying this lesson to the

apostolic age, Israel had been enlightened with Messiah's presence, His miracles and Pentecost with the outpouring of the Holy Spirit, which had given them a heavenly taste. However, they judicially turned back in unbelief. In like manner, God closed the door to national Israel as when He did when they hardened their hearts in Moses' time (*In the provocation in the wilderness*). God had sent national blindness upon them, and told them it was now impossible for those over 20 years of age to enter into Canaan. *If* this passage was in reference to an individual, **that individual could not be renewed if** he had been "**...**once enlightened, and had tasted of the heavenly gift, and was made partakers of the Holy Ghost, And had tasted the good word of God, and the powers of the world to come**...**".Our Arminian brethren have a dilemma here because they teach that a saved person can be unsaved and then be saved again. Again, multiple salvations of the same person are completely alien to the Word of God and are not taught anywhere in the Bible. There is **only one spiritual birth** as well as only one physical birth. Perhaps the reason that our Arminian brethren so *easily* accept the unbiblical dogma of losing salvation is because they presumptuously suppose that they can be saved all over again.

Judicial Israel committed the great sin of rejecting the Holy Spirit's testimony to the risen Messiah. According to Romans chapter 11, they are nationally blinded and cast away until the fullness of the Gentiles be come in. Pentecost had occurred and no one is tasting the powers of the Kingdom Age of Messiah today (*although many claim to duplicate miraculous powers*).

The Sacrifice of Jesus to Expiate Sin Was ONCE and NO MORE

Hebrews 7:27: Who needeth not daily, as those high priests, to offer up sacrifice, first for his own sins, and then for the people's: for this He (Jesus) did ONCE, when He offered up Himself.

I Peter 3:18: "For Christ also hath ONCE suffered for sins..."

Hebrews 9:12: "...but by His own blood He entered in ONCE into the Holy Place, having obtained eternal redemption for us."

Hebrews 9:26: "...but now ONCE in the end of the world hath He appeared to put away sin by the sacrifice of Himself."

Hebrews 10:10: By the which will we are sanctified through the offering of the body of Jesus Christ ONCE for all.

Hebrews 10:12: But this Man (God-man)after He had offered ONE sacrifice for sins for ever, sat down on the right hand of God.

Romans 6:10: For in that He died, He died unto sin ONCE: but in that He liveth, He liveth unto God.

The ONE offering of Christ is phrased in an eternal sense, never to be repeated:

Hebrews 10:14: For by ONE offering He hath perfected FOR EVER them that are sanctified.

Hebrews 10:18: Now where remission of these (sins and iniquities) is, there is NO MORE offering for sin.

Sinners do not deserve the first offering up of Jesus for sin and no one will ever be offered another sacrificial offering of the crucifixion of Christ. A second offering would crucify Jesus afresh, and put Him to an open shame (*Hebrews 6:6*). Christ died for ALL of our sins (*I Corinthians 15:3*) **ONCE,** and there are **NO MORE OFFERINGS** ever (*Hebrews 9:28; 10:18*). Multiple salvations for one person would demand multiple offerings.

102

*Hebrews 9:28: So **Christ was ONCE offered** to bear the sins of many; and unto them that look for Him shall He appear the second time, without sin unto salvation.*

We are looking for Christ, not the antichrist (*Titus 2:13*).

Salvation by Works Refuted by Scriptures

The Bible clearly refutes salvation by works. The holy precepts of Mosaic Law condemned the sinner because the sinner was unable to keep the Law of God perfectly.

Galatians 3:21: Is the law then against the promises of God? God forbid: for if there had been a law given which could have given life, Verily righteousness should have been by the law.

❖ Believers are God's children by faith in Jesus Christ:

*Galatians 3:26: For ye are all the children of God **by faith** in Christ Jesus.*

❖ The law was a curse to us because we could not keep all of its holy precepts:

*Galatians 3:13: Christ hath redeemed us from **the curse of the law**, being made a curse for us: for it is written, Cursed is every one that hangeth on a tree.*

❖ The works of the law do not justify man:

*Galatians 2:16: Knowing that **a man is not justified by the works of the law**, but by the faith of Jesus Christ, **even we have believed in Jesus Christ**, that we might be justified by the **faith of Christ**, and not by the works of the law: for **by the works of the law shall no flesh be justified.***

❖ The works of the law frustrate the grace of God:

103

Galatians 2:21: I do not frustrate the grace of God: for if righteousness come by the law, then Christ is dead in vain.

❖ Believers are not kept saved or made perfect by the flesh:

Galatians 3:3: Are ye so foolish? having begun in the Spirit, are ye now made perfect by the flesh?

❖ A dependence upon works to obtain Heaven is reckoned to be of debt:

Romans 4:4: Now to him that worketh is the reward not reckoned of grace but of debt.

❖ Abraham was justified without works:

*Romans 4:2-3: For **if Abraham were justified by works**, he hath whereof to glory: but not before God. For what saith the Scripture? Abraham **believed***

God and it was counted unto him for righteousness.

❖ David knew that righteousness was imputeth without works:

*Romans 4:6: Even as David also describeth the blessedness of the man, unto whom **God imputeth righteousness without works**.*

❖ Scriptures conclude that **justification is of faith** without law keeping:

Romans 3:28: Therefore we conclude that a man is justified by faith without the deeds of the law.

*Romans 3:27: Where is **boasting then**? It is excluded. By what law? of works? Nay: but by the **law of faith**.*

Works opens the door for boasting. If believers were justified by works for salvation, boasting would **not** be excluded. The verse of I Corinthians 1:29 says that no flesh should glory in His presence. If we could be saved or retain our salvation by any degree of any kind of works, we might put the crown upon our own heads.

❖ Does James say that works are necessary to obtain salvation?

> *James 2:24-25:* **Ye see** *then how that* **by works a man is justified**, *and* **not by faith only**. *Likewise also was not Rahab the harlot* **justified by works**, *when she had received the messengers, and had sent them out another way?*

James is emphasizing the importance of works as a testimony before an unbelieving world. James is **not** saying that works saves. James **is** saying that a genuine Bible faith will produce works. This is the same thing as saying that a faith that does not produce works is a dead faith (*James 2:17, 20*). James makes this quite plain in James 2:18.He says, "...**show me** thy faith without thy works, and I will **shew thee** my faith by my works."

❖ The inferred truth concerning works is given in James 2:18:

✓ There is no true faith that does not produce some degree of works (*within time*)

✓ There is no true faith (*salvation*) by works

James is teaching that a man's faith can only be demonstrated to his fellow man by an outward demonstration of works. God looks upon the heart of man and sees faith, and that faith is counted for righteousness. Too, notice that **justification by works** is not before God, but **before man:** Observe the, show me, of James 2:18 and the, Ye see, of James 2:24. James' concern is that the believer's faith be manifested by his works before his fellowman who can only see the believer's faith as manifested by works. Our salvation is by the supernatural, new birth (*John 3:3-7; I Peter 1:23;*

105

Romans 2:13; Ephesians 2:8, 9; Romans 3:20; Galatians 2:16; 2 Corinthians 5:17).

Does the teaching of James contradict the teaching of Romans?

Definitely not! Rightly divided, no Scripture contradicts another. In Romans 4:2-3, we are plainly told that Abraham **believed** (*faith*) God and it was counted unto him for righteousness. In verse 2, we are told that his works did not justify him **before God**.

In James, we have, **"Ye (***men***) see** then how that **by works a man is justified**, and **not by faith only"** (*James 2:24*). The, Ye, used here, is not God; it is man. In James 2:21, we are told that **Abraham justified his faith by works** when he had offered his son, Isaac, upon the altar. This does not mean that Abraham was saved because he offered up his son as a sacrifice; it meant that Abraham's actions proved or demonstrated his great faith in God. Abraham was already a justified man because of his faith in God, **before** offering up Isaac, his son. It would not be expected of God to ask an ungodly sinner to offer up a son. Only the offering of God's Son, Jesus, could justify a sinner. The context is **not** that of Abraham coming as an unbeliever to offer his son as a sacrifice so that he might obtain salvation by works. Too, God also immediately countermanded this very unusual test of faith, which He had commanded of Abraham. We are told in the New Testament that Abraham had great **faith** that God was able to raise Isaac up, even from the dead:

> *Hebrews 11:19: Accounting that God was able to raise him* (Isaac) *up, even from the dead; from whence also He received him in a figure.*

James is not contradicting what Paul said in Romans chapter 4. Paul is laying down the "principle" of salvation. James is showing "the working" of that principle in the believer's life, a faith that produces works.

James himself expressly states that Abraham **believed** (*faith*) God, and it was **imputed** (*charged*) unto him for righteousness (*James 2:23*).

Works can only **validate** (*confirm; verify*) true faith; works **cannot produce** salvation:

Salvation is Secure

- Salvation is a **gift** (*not an earned wage*) through faith alone and never deserved.

- Salvation is **by God's grace (**independent of any merit or good works).

- **Man at his very best falls short** of the glory of God (*Romans 3:23*) and would, in the end, have to forfeit salvation, **if** *(hypothetically)* it could be forfeited; therefore if any man is ever finally saved at all, it must be all of God's power and grace, both the saving and the keeping.

- The life received upon salvation is never temporary but always **everlasting life.** Salvation is never limited to being conditional upon works or faithfulness.

- Although the believer's faith will be tried (*I Peter 1:7*), salvation is NOT conditioned upon maintaining good works. A saved person is never given over to a probationary salvation. Salvation is an unconditional covenant.

- The believer is **already sitting together in heavenly places** in Christ Jesus **(***Ephesians 2:6***).**

- The believer is **presently glorified** (*Romans 8:30*) according to the foreknowledge (*omniscience*) and omnipotence (*power*) of God (*Ephesians 1:45*).

- We are not saved because we are good (*there is none good, no not one*) and we are not lost because we are bad. We are saved by trusting Christ (*Matthew 22:42; 2 Corinthians 5:17*), and being born again (*John 3:3-7; I Peter 1:23*).

- The new man (spiritual man) cannot sin (*I John 3:9 – "practice a life-style of lawlessness or iniquity"*). This new man is a new creature *(2 Corinthians 5:17)*.

- A saved person **cannot be** unborn and neither can he be re-born over and over again.

- No one that has passed from spiritual death unto spiritual life (*John 5:24*) has ever, nor ever will, revert back to spiritual death from spiritual life.

- A born-again person **can never die spiritually,** nor can he corrupt because the believer's new birth is of **incorruptible seed (***I Peter 1:23; John 1:12, 13)*.

- A born-again person is saved by grace through faith, and is **kept by the power of God** (*I Peter 1:5; Psalms 121:5*). The believer is not kept by human merits, such as righteous works, faithfulness, good deeds, virtues or "so called" sacraments.

- If a saint sins, he has **an Advocate with the Father**, Jesus, who is the propitiation (reconciliation) for our sins (*I John 2:1-2*). It is never said that a believer that sins becomes

108

unsaved or that he is urged to be saved again (*hypothetically, of course*).

- **The Lord will not impute (**charge; attribute**) sin to those whose iniquities are forgiven** (*Romans 4:5-8*).

- The children of the devil's kingdom are translated from the power of darkness into the kingdom of God's dear Son *(Colossians 1:13*), but God's children (*Romans 8:16, 21; Galatians 3:26*) are never reverted back to become a child of Hell (*Matthew 23:15*).

- "**...**he that doeth the will of God abideth forever" (*I John 2:17*).

- -Doing the will of God is embracing the Gospel of Christ, which is believing (*faith*) on the Son (*John 6:27-29; 6:37-40; I John 4:4; 5:4, 5*). The **new birth** is the will of God toward man.

Three Births are mentioned in the Bible:

1. **Physical birth:** The physical birth of man (*Job 5:7; John 3:4, 6*).

2. **New Birth:** Because of sin, a spiritual birth, the new birth, is essential for becoming a citizen of the Kingdom of God (*John 3:3, 5, 7; I Peter 1:23; I Corinthians 12:13*). There is never a second, or third spiritual birth mentioned at all.

3. **Virgin Birth:** The other birth is **the virgin birth** of Jesus, our **Saviour** (*Isaiah 7:14; Matthew1:23; Luke 1:27-35: Jeremiah 31:22; Genesis 3:15*).-Of course, the virgin birth of Christ was miraculous, even though it was a natural birth. The greater miracle was in the **conception** of Christ of the Holy Ghost.

- Nowhere in the Bible is divine nature (*2 Peter 1:4*) removed from a believer.

- **Christ died for ALL my sins**, past, present, and future. Christ did not die just for past sins alone. ALL of the saints sins were **future sins** when Christ died.

- Whosoever drinks of the water that Jesus gives him shall **never thirst** (*John 4:14*). **If** (*hypothetically*) he could become unsaved, he would thirst again.

- He that comes to the bread of life shall **never hunger** (*John 6:35*). Of course, this is speaking of the spiritual hunger of eternal life (*salvation*), not physical bread. True believers have suffered physical hunger in the past and others may suffer hunger in the future (*Revelation 13:17*). This spiritual hunger is in reference to Jesus, The Bread of Life, not food (*John 6:32, 48, 51*).

- **God is able to succour** them that are tempted (*Hebrews 2:18*). Of course, some readily confess that God is able but erroneously suppose that He will not always.

- **A just man** may fall seven times, but he **riseth up again** (*Proverbs 24:16*).

- (The definite number seven, which is the number of perfection and completion, is given for an indefinite number of times of rising up again.)

- **We are more than conquerors** through Him that loved us (*Romans 8:37*).

- **He is able to keep you from falling** and to present you faultless (*Jude 24*).

(It does not say that He is able but not always willing.)

- **Whosoever** believeth in Him should not perish (*John 3:16*).

- Our life is **hid with Christ** in God (*Satan cannot find us*) - Colossians 3:3.

- The **Good Shepherd has the responsibility** of keeping the sheep (*Psalms 121:5; John 10:11-14; Matthew 18:10-14; I Peter 1:5*). Some claim to be their own shepherd.

- He that believeth on Him is **not condemned** (*John 3:18*).

- -Nowhere is it stated that the saved might be or could be condemned with the world. However, the Scriptures do state that believers may be chastened of the Lord, but they will not be condemned with the world (*I Corinthians 11:32*).

- He that is born again **abideth forever** (*I Peter 1:23*).

(If only one saved person could become unsaved, this verse would not be true.)

- The **believer's hope is preserved** and will not fade away (*I Peter 1:4-5*).

- The believer's **inheritance is incorruptible** (*I Peter 1:4*).

Our eternal inheritance (*Hebrews 9:15*) is undefiled, pure, un-decaying, immortal, and cannot die. God is able to keep our soul (*2 Timothy 1:12*).

- **None** are lost that Christ prays for (*John 17:9-12*). Christ does everything according to the will of His Father (*John 5:19; Hebrews 10:7; I John 5:14, 15*). The prayer of Jesus for the believer's salvation will be answered (*Hebrews 7:25*).

- Whosoever liveth and believeth in Christ **shall never die** (*spiritually*) - John 11:26.(It is appointed unto man once to die physically – Hebrews 9:37.)

- The believer will **in no wise be cast out** under any circumstances (*John 6:37*). This is in reference to a former sinner that had been saved by trusting in Christ salvation, not of a sinner coming to Christ for salvation and being rejected. Neither will a repentant sinner be rejected.

- **None that the Father gives to Jesus will He lose** and will raise him up again at the last day (*John 6:39*).

- There is **nothing or no one in life or in death** that can separate believers from the love of God (*Romans 8:35-39*).

- The Holy Spirit **abides forever** inside the saved person (*John 14:16-17; 16:13*).

- Saints are **seated with Christ** (*Ephesians 2:4*-6). A believer is never unseated.

- The Lord's saints **ARE preserved forever** (*Psalms 37:38; 121:7; 2 Timothy 4:18; Jude 1:1*). It is not, will be preserved.

- **Jesus is the Author (Origin) and the Finisher (Securer; Sustainer) of our faith** (*Hebrews 12:2*). Works are essential after salvation; However, **Works cannot keep that which it could not begin.**

Jesus started our salvation and He will finish it. Nothing can be taken away nor anything added to it (*such as, holding out*).

- The blood of Jesus Christ blots out sin but sin never blots out the blood.

- The giving of the Holy Spirit is an **Earnest, Seal,** and a **Promise** to believers

(2 Corinthians 5:1-2, 5; Ephesians 1:13, 14; Acts 1:4-5, 8; Ephesians 1:13; 4:30).

1. The word, earnest (*Greek "arrhabon"*), is equivalent to the OT word, pledge (*arabown*) - Genesis 38:17-20. Some like to say, the down-payment that secures the principal. Nowhere in Scripture does God renege on His pledge, or His promise of everlasting salvation. God has already **sealed us** and given the pledge of the Spirit in our hearts. What God said is true; what God promises, He will do.

> 2 Corinthians 1:20-22: For **all the promises** of God in Him are **yea**, and in Him **Amen**, unto the glory of God by us. Now He which stablisheth us with you in Christ, and hath anointed us, is God: Who hath also **sealed us**, and **given the earnest of the Spirit** in our hearts.

- The Father reckons saints to be:
  - ➢ Baptized into Christ (*I Corinthians 12:13*)
  - ➢ Dead with Christ (*Galatians 2:20; 3:3*)
  - ➢ Buried with Christ (*Romans 6:4*)

113

> ➤ Raised with Christ (*Ephesians 2:6*)

> ➤ Seated with Christ (*Ephesians 2:6*)

- The Lord knoweth how to deliver the godly out of temptations (*2 Peter 2:9*)

- For in that He Himself hath suffered being tempted, He is able to succour them *(*believers*)* that are tempted (*Hebrews 2:18*)

- Though he *(believer)* fall, he shall **not be utterly cast down** for the Lord upholdeth him with His hand (*Psalms 37:24-25*).

The believer can definitely fall in salvation, but he cannot fall out of salvation.

- But the salvation of the righteous is of the Lord: He is their strength in the time of trouble. And the Lord shall help them, and deliver them: He shall deliver them from the wicked, and save them, because they trust in Him (*Psalms 37:39-40*)

Just as no believer can save himself, so no believer can keep himself.

- We are dead to sin (*Romans 6:2*). The spiritual man, who is born of God, doth not commit sin (*continually live a rebellious, sinful life-style*) for His seed remaineth in him: and he cannot sin, because he is born of God (*I John 3:9*)

We cannot hope to trust in maintaining good works for our righteousness.

- And whosoever liveth and believeth in Me shall **never die**. Believeth thou this?- (*John 11:26*)

It is appointed to men once to die a physical death (*Hebrews 9:27*), but believers shall never die the Second Death of the lake of fire (*Revelation 20:6*)

• For by ONE offering He hath **perfected forever** them that are sanctified (*Hebrews 10:12, 14*)

All believers are sanctified forever by God's Son, Jesus (John 17:19; Acts 20:32; 26:18; I Corinthians 1:2; 6:11; Hebrews 2:11; 10:10, 14).

When Does Everlasting Life Begin?

Everlasting/eternal life begins the very moment that a person is saved (born again):

*I John 3:2: Beloved, **now** are we the sons of God, and it doth not yet appear what we shall be: but we know that, when He shall appear, we shall be like Him; for we shall see Him as He is.*

*John 5:24: Verily, verily, I say unto you, He (whosoever) that heareth My word, and believeth on Him (God) that sent Me, **hath** (present possession) everlasting life, and **shall not** (settled future) come into condemnation; but **is passed** (finished transaction) from death unto life.*

*John 10:28: And I **give** (present tense verb denoting continuance) unto them eternal life; and they shall **never perish** (definite declaration), neither shall any man (entity; power) pluck them out of My hand.*

As seen in these verses of Scripture, eternal life is a **present possession** and not a conditional salvation. The believer's hope (Gk. *elpis*) express certainty and in anticipation Eternal life begins with the new birth and remains during and through physical life, continues through physical death, and wondrously metamorphoses into a glorified body to **never end** (*John 3:3, 5, 7, 16, 18*). Again, a temporary, probationary, or conditional

115

salvation is never taught in the Bible. God only gives eternal life.

More than 45 times the terms, "Eternal Life" and "Everlasting Life," appear in the NT.

ETERNAL LIFE EVERLASTING LIFE

Matthew 25:46	Matthew 19:29
John 3:15	John 3:16, 36
John 6:54, 58	John 4:14
John 10:28	John 5:24
John 17:2, 3	John 6:27, 40, 47
Acts 13:48	Acts 13:46
Romans 5:21	Galatians 6:8
Romans 6:23	I Timothy 1:16
Titus 1:2; 3:7	Hebrews 9:12
I John. 2:25; 5:11, 13	Galatians 6:8

Other various synonymous terms are used in reference to eternal life, such as: eternal redemption; eternal glory; eternal salvation; and eternal inheritance.

God **gives a** penitent sinner the unconditional **gift of Eternal Life** (*Romans 6:23*); however, **rewards, crowns,** and special **blessings** are conditional and dependent upon faithful stewardship, service, and soul-winning.

116

If this writer could become lost after being saved over 50 years, he did not receive eternal life; again, God promised eternal life, not just life.

The dogmas and commandments of men are not reliable (*Matthew 15:9; Mark 7:7; Colossians 2:22*).

Believers are **not kept** by their own power:

*I Peter 1:5: Who are **kept** by the power of God, through faith, unto salvation ready to be revealed in the last time.*

Jesus prayed that the Father would **keep those** that His Father had given Him (*John 17:11*). Again, what part of **keep** or **kept** by the power of God, do our Arminian brethren not understand?

Not only is God able to keep His children (*2 Timothy 1:12*), but He promises that He is willing to **keep** them.

In plain English, a person cannot live holy enough to pave their road to Heaven. Jesus paid the full price for sin at Calvary and anything man adds to God's sacrifice of His Darling Son is void (*empty; useless*). Men's works to obtain salvation is only futility in progress. However, believers should strive to be holy in all their works (*Ephesians 1:4; 5:27; 2 Timothy 1:9: I Peter 1:15-16*). Without God's imparted holiness, no man shall see the Lord (*Hebrews 12:14*).

Jesus plainly settled the matter of *Eternal Life* for His sheep:

*John 10:27-30: **My sheep** hear My voice, and I know them, and they follow Me: And **I give unto them eternal life**: and **they shall never perish** (a promise), neither shall any man (entity; power) pluck them out of My hand. My Father, which gave them Me, is greater than all; and no man is able to*

117

pluck them out of My Father's hand. I and My Father are one.

The, they that shall never perish, applies to Jesus' sheep upon earth, not in Heaven.

Unbelief Is the Final Doom of Unrepentant Sinners

*Isaiah 33:14: "...**Who** among us shall dwell with the devouring fire? **who** among us shall dwell with **everlasting burnings**?*

*Isaiah 66:24: And they shall go forth, and look upon the carcases of the men that transgressed against Me: for **their worm shall not die**, **neither shall their fire be quenched**; and they shall be an abhorring unto all flesh.*

*Matthew 18:8: Wherefore if thy hand or thy foot offend thee, cut them off, and cast them from thee: it is better for thee to enter into life halt or maimed, rather than having two hands or two feet to be cast into **everlasting fire*** (in a body of sorts).

*Matthew 25:41: Then shall He say also unto them on the left hand, Depart from Me, ye cursed, into **everlasting fire** prepared for the devil and his angels: (What would be the purpose of an empty everlasting fire without any inhabitants?)*

Matthew 25:46: And these (unbelievers) *shall go away into **everlasting punishment**: but the righteous into life eternal.*

*Mark 9:43-48: And if thy hand offend thee, cut it off: it is better for thee to enter into life maimed, than having two hands to go into hell into **the fire that never shall be quenched**: Where **their worm dieth not**, and the **fire is not quenched**...to be cast into hell into **the fire that never shall be quenched**:...Where **their worm dieth not**, and the* *fire is not quenched....Where **their worm dieth not, and the fire is not quenched**.*

*II Thessalonians 1:9: Who shall be punished with **everlasting destruction** from the presence of the Lord, and from the glory of his power.*

*Revelation 20:13-14: And the sea gave up the dead which were in it; and death and hell delivered up the dead which were in them: and they were judged every man according to their works. And death and hell were **cast into the lake of fire**. This is **the second death**.*

*Revelation 21:8: But the fearful, and **unbelieving**, and the abominable, and murders, and whoremongers, and sorcerers, and idolaters, and all liars, shall have their part in **the lake which burneth with fire and brimstone**: which is **the second death**.*

Committing the worst kind of sin is not the greatest threat to the loss of a man's soul. **Unbelief is the worst sin of all** (*Hebrews 3:12*). There is **no** forgiveness for unbelief; Unbelief is **an unpardonable sin**.

Unbelief of God's Word Is Calling God a Liar

*I John 5:10-13: He that believeth on the Son of God hath the witness in himself: **he that believeth not God hath made Him a liar**; because he **believeth not the record** that God gave of His Son. And **this is the record, that God hath given to us eternal life**, and this life is in His Son. **He that hath the Son hath life**; and he that hath not the Son of God hath not life. These things have I written unto you that believe on the name of the Son of God; **that ye may know that ye have eternal life**, and that ye may believe on the name of the Son of God.*

*Romans 14:23: And he that **doubteth** is damned if he eat, because he eateth not of **faith**: for **whatsoever is not of faith is sin**.*

Rebellious and Unbelieving Sinners Are Paving Their Road to Hell

In Corinthians 6:9-11, we have the good news that many of the vilest of sinners had come to salvation. These had formerly been fornicators, idolaters, adulterers, effeminate (sodomite; homosexual), thieves, and drunkards, but no longer. The worst kinds of sin can be forgiven (murder; abortion; sodomy; bestiality (human/animal sexual relation - Leviticus 18:22, 23; I Corinthians 6:9-11). However, there is hope for all sinners. The sin of unbelief cannot be forgiven (John 3:18, 36).

The Good News of the gospel of Christ is that ALL of the most evil sinners can be forgiven, "And such were some of you: but ye are washed, but ye are sanctified, but ye are justified in the name of the Lord Jesus, and by the Spirit of our God" (*I Corinthians 6:11*). Being washed means that you no longer practice a lifestyle of former sins (*2 Corinthians 5:17; I John 3:9*). In this present evil world, it is politically correct to christianize liars, thieves, adulterers, fornicators, abortionists and sodomites. Phony religionists are sanitizing all kinds of filthy sin.

*John 3:18: He that believeth on Him is not condemned: but **he that believed not is condemned already**, because he hath not believed in the name of the only begotten Son of God.*

Eternal Life Is Eternal Security

There are no verses or texts in the entire Bible that teach that a saved person can become unsaved, but there are verses and texts that are twisted out of context and misconstrued as such. There are numerous verses and texts in the Bible that are crystal clear concerning salvation and the security of the believer.

False doctrines come into being by religious people falsely interpreting Bible texts or verses that **appear** to imply something that the context will not allow. Clever spin-doctors (spin-meisters) twist Scriptures to agree with their private dogmas.

In the matter of salvation, there are no indecisive or middle positions with God. It is a 100 % certainty that a saved person cannot become unsaved or it is a 100 % certainty that a saved person can become unsaved (*no half-way house*).

Some falsely contend that there is a second chance for salvation after death. They suppose that there is a limbo state (*neutral ground*) or a purgatory (*invention of man*) awaiting them. However, man in his day of grace has neglected thousands of opportunities (*seconds. minutes; hours; days; weeks; months; years*) for salvation and there will be no "so called' second chances after death. It only takes a moment in time to trust in Jesus.

The writer came to the Lord to receive **eternal life** that he had heard much about, not to be saved and then be "allegedly" lost again. After much Bible study, the writer became thoroughly convinced of the assurance of Heaven as explicitly expressed by the gift of eternal life.

Doubters of Eternal Life

The writer believes that a major reason that people are so easily deceived over the question of the believer's security is because there are so many *unsaved* church members. Many religiously oriented people have made a pretense of salvation, served in the church for a while and then went out again to their old lifestyle of sin. These false professions by unsaved church members have bred doubts for many.

Another reason that our Arminian brethren reject the Bible doctrine of eternal life can be traced to their excessive reliance upon feelings and emotions that often vary and are unreliable. We are admonished to walk by faith, not by sight. Arminian brethren often interpret the Bible by human experiences and emotions rather than trusting the Bible in understanding experiences and emotions.

Works are the Subtle Entrapment of the Soul

*At the future White Throne judgment, **unsaved religious Pharisees and church members** will plead their case before God on the basis of their many wonderful works.*

*Matthew 7:22-23: **Many** will say to Me in that day, Lord, Lord, have we not **prophesied in Thy name?** and in Thy name have **cast out devils?** and **in Thy name done many wonderful works**? And then will I profess unto them, **I never knew you**: depart from Me, ye that work iniquity.*

Notice that the Lord does not say that I once knew you, but no more. Jesus said that He **never** knew them at all. Neither does Jesus deny their claims of **prophesying, casting out devils, and doing wonderful works**. Either they really did those things (*it appears that Judas might have done so – Mark 6:7, 13*), or their claims were not worthy of an answer by the Lord. It is no surprise that these unsaved religious sinners laid claim to many wonderful works in Jesus' name in order to justify themselves. What is stunning is that these vain, self-righteous pleas, were **in the very presence of God.** They were handed over to the angels to be cast into a furnace of fire - (*Matthew 13:41-42, 50; 25:41*).

122

Scriptures plainly teach that salvation *is a* gift of God without works *(Ephesians 2:8-10; Galatians 2:16; Romans 4:4-6, 20)*. Considering that lost men will plead their good works **before God** at the White Throne judgment, it should be no surprise to us that church members lay claim to salvation by good works **in the presence of their fellow man.**

Another surprising matter at the White Throne judgment is that of the unsaved religionists boasting confidently of their works to justify themselves. This is surprising when you consider that many saved brethren live a life of doubting their salvation.

Jesus told the **outwardly clean** religious Pharisees who tithed, fasted twice a week, and had good works (*of outward show*) that they were not fit for Heaven (*Luke 18:12; Matthew 23:23*).

> *Matthew 23:27-28: Woe unto you, scribes and Pharisees, hypocrites! for ye are like unto whited sepulchres, which indeed* ***appear beautiful outward****, but are within full of dead men's bones, and of all uncleanness. Even so ye also* ***outwardly appear righteous unto men****, but within* ***ye are full of hypocrisy and iniquity****.*

In Matthew chapter 23, Jesus pronounced **woes** upon these unsaved religious leaders. He called them **hypocrites** (*stage actors; pretenders of true religion*), blind guides, fools, serpents, vipers, and children of them which killed the prophets. So much for some religious leaders and their blind followers!

The hypocrite does not persevere in true religion very long because he has no pleasure in it; it becomes a drudgery and weariness to him.

Bible Verses/Texts Alleged to Support the Arminian View

John 15:1-8: *I AM the true vine, and My Father is the husbandman. Every branch* **in Me** *that beareth not fruit He taketh away: and every branch that beareth* **fruit***, He purgeth it, that is may bring forth* **more fruit***. Now ye are clean through the word which I have spoken unto you. Abide in Me, and I in you. As the branch cannot* **bear fruit** *of itself, except it abide in the vine; no more can ye, except ye abide in Me. I am the vine, ye are the branches: He that abideth* **in Me***, and I in him, the same bringeth forth* **much fruit***: for without Me ye can do nothing.* **If a man abide not in Me***, he is cast forth as a branch, and is withered; and men gather them, and cast them into the fire, and they are burned.* **If ye abide in Me***, and My words abide in you, ye shall ask what ye will, and it shall be done unto you. Herein is My Father glorified, that ye bear* **much fruit***; so shall ye be My disciples.*

A casual reading might lead the reader to believe that these verses are alluding to a saved person that becomes unsaved because he did not abide in the Lord. A closer look at the context clearly states that the subject is, **abiding in Christ for fruit bearing**, not abiding in Christ to get to Heaven. The text is saying that a branch in Christ that that does **not** abide in fellowship with Christ is powerless. The branch, i**n Christ,** that does not bear fruit is taken away. This appears to be a partial answer to the sin unto death of I John 5:16 and Romans 6:16, This branch, **in Me**, that does not produce fruit is **likened to** a withered branch that does not produce fruit and is worthless for service, and consequently burned in the fire. However, it is dead branches (*not men*) that do not produce fruit that are thrown into the fire by men to burn. It is not believers, **in Me** (Christ), that do not produce fruit that are thrown in the fire to burn. Too, itis angels, not men, who cast lost men into Hell (*Matthew 113:41-42*).If saved people could become lost and then be thrown into the fire of Hell, surely the Scriptures would plainly say so. Again, the text is concerned with, **degrees of fruit bearing and the necessity of abiding in Christ to do so.** Observe that the branches that, beareth not fruit, are also included in the branches **in Me (***All four groups were branches in Christ -John 15:2***)** Obviously, not all of those **in Christ** bore fruit. Others abiding in the love of Christ bore fruit at different degrees (*John 15:1-2, 4, 7-8, 10, 16*). The degrees of fruit-bearing are given as, beareth **not fruit** (*John 15:2)*, beareth **fruit** (John 15:2), bring forth **more fruit** (*John 15:2*), and bear **much fruit** (*John 15:5, 8*). Those that bore no fruit were in Christ.

Of the branch, in Me (Christ), that beareth not fruit, we are told that, He (God) taketh away (*John 15:2*). We are not told why the branch in Me did not produce fruit. Again, perhaps, the unfruitful branch in Christ is in reference to a sin unto death of a sinning, disobedient Christian who is not willing to serve or abide in Christ for whatever reason (*John 15:2; Romans 6:16; I John 5:16*).

The thief on the cross did not have time to bear any appreciable fruit, yet Jesus said, Today shalt thou be with Me in Paradise (*Luke 23:43*). An innocent child that dies before their age of accountability, does not bear any fruit at all, and yet they are received into Heaven. Sin is not imputed (charged; attributed) to an innocent child for inherent sin of his physical birth (adamic nature), and it goes to Heaven when it dies (*The exact age and time of accountability of a young child is known only to God*). David said of his deceased child, "...I shall go to him, but he shall not return to me" (*2 Samuel 12:23*). Of course, we know that David was a true believer who went to Paradise (*Heaven*). Some adult babes in Christ have died soon after they were saved and had little or no time to bear fruit (*as in death bed repentance*). The lack of fruit or the degree of fruit produced by a believer does not determine whether or not that person will enter Heaven. A sinner has to be born again to escape the judgment of Hell (*John 3:3, 5, 7; I Peter 1:23; 2 Corinthians 5:17*). Jesus Himself said that the new birth is absolutely essential for entrance into the kingdom of God.

◆ ***John 13:8:*** *Peter saith unto Him, Thou shalt never wash my feet. Jesus answered him, If I wash thee not, thou hast no part with Me.*

The Lord used this occasion to teach His disciples an important spiritual lesson. Unless

God's children are willing to accept God's offer of **frequent cleansing**, they have no part with Him in **fellowship, service, and fruitbearing**. Notice that the verse does not say no part **in Me** (as being damned), but no part **with me** (in fellowship; fruitbearing). We are **once bathed** (salvation) and need only **wash thereafter** (daily cleansing of confession).

See John 4:10, 13-14; 7:38; 13:9-10; I John 1:9; Ephesians 5:26; Numbers chapter 19.

◆ ***Matthew 12:43-45:*** *When the unclean spirit is gone out of a man, he walketh through dry places, seeking rest, and findeth none. Then he saith, I will return into **my house** from whence I came out; and when he is come, he findeth it **empty**, swept, and garnished. Then goeth he, and taketh with himself seven other spirits more wicked than himself, and they enter in and dwell there: and the last state of that man is worse than the first. Even so shall it be also unto this wicked generation.*

This is not a picture of a saved man becoming unsaved. Here, the unclean spirit goes out of his own decision, he is not driven out by the Holy Spirit, who resides in a saint. The Holy Spirit does not share the same body or tabernacle with demonic spirits. Notice also

126

that when the wicked spirit returns to **his house,** he finds that it is **empty;** again, a believer's house is not empty because he is **indwelt with the Holy Spirit** of promise (*John 7:39; 14:16, 17; 16:7-14; Acts 1:8; 2:16; Corinthians 6:19; 2 Corinthians 1:21-22; Ephesians 1:13-14; 4:30; I John 2:20-27; Romans 8:9*). The house in this text still belonged to the unclean spirit (*my house, Hebrews 12:44*).

This is a picture of a person who has experienced some degree of **reformation** as indicated by the terms, empty, swept, and garnished (*adorned; decorated; embellished*). This person had not been truly purged of his sinful condition and was only clean on the outside. The house was only swept (*reformed*), it was not bathed clean (*salvation*). Only the exterior dust was removed. This typifies a Pharisee type of person who is trusting in his own self-righteousness and outward goodness. Jesus likened the pretentious, self-righteous, hypocritical Pharisee to a whited sepulchre, who was only washed (*white-washed*) on the outside, not clean on the inside.

A man trusting in his own reformation opens himself up to even more demonic control. This is indicated by the **seven other spirits more wicked** than himself that the wicked spirit brought back with him to **his** house.

> *Matthew 5:20: For I say unto you, That except your righteousness shall exceed the righteousness of the scribes and Pharisees, ye shall in no case enter into the kingdom of Heaven.*

> *Matthew 21:31: "...the publicans and the harlots go into the kingdom of God before you" (chief priests; elders; hypocrites).*

> ◆ *Matthew 10:22: And ye shall be hated of all men for My name's sake: but he that **endureth to the end** shall be saved (also refer to Matthew 24:13).*

127

In order to understand this verse, it is necessary to determine the context and realize what end is meant (this is the end of The Great Tribulation) and just what kind of salvation is referred to (this is the saving of the flesh). To some, this might *appear* to say that one must hold out, or to endure faithfully to the end of life in order to go to Heaven. However, salvation of the soul is not in view at all in this text. This speaks of the person's physical life (or flesh) during global judgments. The he that endureth to the end of the 7-Year Tribulation Period are those saved Jews (and Gentiles), who endure the great judgments upon the earth and are saved. They will have their lives (flesh) saved at Christ's Second Coming. From the prophecy of Zechariah 13:8, 9, it appears that two-thirds of Israel will die during this future time of the Great Tribulation. The scene is during Daniel's 70th Week of Prophecy (*Daniel 9:24-27*). In the OT, this period of time is also called the time of Jacob's trouble (*Jeremiah 30:7*). The Great Tribulation is the last 3 1/2 years of the 7-Year Tribulation Period which will end with the coming of Christ as Lord of lords and King of kings. The subject is **salvation of the flesh,** not the soul. Matthew 24:22 says of that time, except those days should be shortened, there should no **flesh** be saved. Saved Jews and Gentles that, endure to the end, of The Great Tribulation (Daniel's 70th Week) will enter alive into the Millennial reign of Christ. Daniel's 70th Week of Prophecy will end at the Second Coming of Christ to earth.

Hitler's holocaust will appear but as a small thing when compared to the destruction upon earth and decimation of Israel's number during The Great Tribulation. This will be such a time as was not since the beginning of the world to this time, no, nor ever shall be. Jesus is telling the saved Jews (and believing Gentiles) that if they endure to the end of these horrendous judgments upon the world (*Revelation 12:12; 16:1*), their lives (*flesh)* will be saved. He that endureth to the end of the Great Tribulation will be saved at Christ's Second Coming (*Revelation 7:9*).

◆ *I Corinthians 9:27: But I keep under my body and bring it into subjection: lest that by any means, when I have preached to others, I myself should be a **castaway***.

Paul is not saying that he fears that he would lose his salvation. The word, castaway, is from the Greek word, *adokinos,* meaning, not approved, disqualified, or rejected. **The subject here is service,** or not approved for service. It is not Paul's salvation that may be disqualified for he is saying that his **ministry** could be disapproved of God if he did not keep under his body (*fleshly desires*) and bring it into subjection.

Many preachers today are not qualified to continue in leadership roles of the ministry because of their spiritual weakness and inability to put their flesh in subjection. A sinning leader is not qualified to continue as pastor, bishop, teacher, or evangelist and should be set on the shelf or set aside as a castaway. He is no longer blameless(*I Timothy 3:2*).

The Apostle Paul admits that sin reigned in his body of flesh (*Romans 7:13-20*), but he daily kept it in subjection. Numerous preachers have failed to keep their bodies in subjection and their secret sins have come to light; these religious leaders, that are prone to be led of the flesh, should be ruled disqualified as a presiding leader (bishop; elder). Elders and Bishops must be without blame (*I Timothy 3:1-7*).

Paul appeals to this Church at Corinth on the basis of their knowledge of the athletic games. He mentions that all run in a race but one receiveth the prize (reward). Paul admonishes them, So run, that ye may obtain (*I Corinthians 9:24*). Paul in not expressing concern over retaining his salvation, but winning the prize, his **reward**.

129

By comparing salvation to winning an Olympian prize, Paul says in Romans 9:16, So then it is not of him that willeth, **nor of him that runneth**, but of God that showeth mercy. Salvation is not earned by running, but by God's grace and mercy.

◆ **Galatians 5:4:** *Christ is become of no effect unto you, whosoever of you are justified by the law; ye are **fallen from grace**.*

This verse is not in reference to a saved person "allegedly" becoming unsaved. Many of these Galatians had been saved through faith in the crucified Christ under Paul's preaching, but later had been persuaded by legalistic Jewish teachers that they needed to add the works of the law to Christ's work (*Acts 15:1, 5, 24*). Paul is not saying that these foolish Galatians had lost their salvation for he continues to call them, brethren (*If brethren simply meant brothers in the flesh, it was still a warning to unsaved Jews not to trust in keeping the law for obtaining salvation*).Again, this is in reference to the brethren who would wrongly add the works of the law to saving Grace (*Galatians 2:16*).Grace and works cannot be mixed or mingled (*Romans 11:6*). Salvation is ALL of Grace. When anyone counts his own righteousness (*Isaiah 64:6: Romans 3:10, 23*), such as law-keeping, Christ is become of no effect unto him (*no one is able to keep the whole law*). The person who trusts in keeping the law for salvation has, fallen from grace (*or, the doctrine of grace*) and is resting upon the works of the law (*Galatians 2: 21, 16; 3:3; 10, 12, 13, 21, 26; 4:5; Romans 4:4-6*). Fallen from grace is not falling out of grace.

The New Testament grace of Christ is a **better way** (*economy; system*) than the Old Testament economy of tedious law-keeping (*2 Corinthians 3:6-18; Hebrews 7:19, 22; 8:6-13; 9:11*).Believers are safe in Jesus, the one Who kept all of the law.

◆ *Philippians 2:12: Wherefore, my **beloved**, as ye have always obeyed, not as in my presence only, but now much more in my absence, **work out your own salvation** with fear and trembling.*

Obviously, Paul is not talking about working to *obtaining* salvation here, for he is talking to those that are **already saved.** He calls them my beloved and also lauds them for their continued obedience (*which would not apply to an unsaved person*). Salvation is theirs as a present possession. Neither is Paul admonishing saved people to work to retain salvation. Paul is saying whether in my presence only and much more in my absence, work **outwardly** the salvation of yours that is **inward.**

Again, believers are not told to work for salvation; they are told to work out salvation received entirely by grace. It is not faith plus works, but grace through faith ((Ephesians 2:8; Titus 3:5). We can no more keep our salvation than we can earn it. We (believers) need to show our faith by our works (James 2:18). God has ordained that we should walk in good works (Ephesians 2:10).

◆ *Hebrews 10:26: For if we sin wilfully after that we have received the knowledge of the truth, there remaineth no more sacrifice for sins.*

It is necessary to understand that receiving the knowledge of the truth does not necessarily mean that all of these individuals were saved. This is not a reference to a Christian that sins and "allegedly" loses his salvation. This is in reference to God's covenant with Israel whereby Israel was sanctified (*Hebrews 10:29*).All the Hebrew sacrifices of the Old Testament were reminders of this New Testament covenant of grace (*Jeremiah 31:31, 33*) and all of the sacrifices looked forward to the coming Savior. Although the **unbelieving Jews** received knowledge of Jesus, many stopped short of accepting Him

131

as their sacrifice for sin. This verse was a warning to unbelieving Jews (and Gentiles) who had counted Christ's blood to be common blood as the blood of other men.

The verse is also saying that those who **willfully** reject Christ cannot find any other sacrifice to take away their sin. Israel, as a nation, had judicially crucified Christ afresh by rejecting His once-for-all sacrifice, and turning back to the sacrifices of the law. When the Jews willfully rejected the sacrifice of Christ for their sin, there was no other sacrifice to which they could turn. Having no sacrifice for sin, the Israelite had nothing to anticipate but fiery indignation and judgment. In the same text only a few verses later (*Hebrews 10:39*), the writer of Hebrews proceeds to refer to the **believing Jews** who are not of them (unbelieving Jews) who draw back unto perdition.

Christ alone is our sacrifice for sin. There is **no other sacrifice** to take away the sin of a Jew or Gentile.

(**Note:** The **Old Testament sacrifices did not take away sin;** they **only atoned or covered** sin for a time and had to be often repeated, once every year. Refer to Hebrews 7:11, 19, 27; 8:13; 9:12, 28; 10:4, 10, 14, 17, 20. Jesus appeared **ONCE** to **put away** [*expiate; propitiate; reconcile; put in the right relationship*] the believer's sin forever. Jesus obtained **eternal redemption** [eternal life] for His saints by the sacrifice of Himself (*Hebrews 9:12, 26*.)

Many times in the Scriptures, we are told that Jesus died only **Once** for sin and **No More**:

Romans 6:9-10: Knowing that Christ being raised from the dead **dieth no more**; death hath no more dominion over Him. For in that He died, **He died unto sin once**: but in that He liveth, He liveth unto God

There is only one physical birth and there is only one spiritual birth.

◆ *Hebrews 6:4-6: For it is **impossible** for those who were once enlightened, and have tasted of the heavenly gift, and were made partakers of the Holy Ghost, And have tasted the good word of God, and the powers of the world to come, **If** they shall fall away, to renew them again unto repentance; seeing they crucify to themselves the Son of God afresh, and put Him to an open shame.*

If (*hypothetically*) saved people could fall away (*lose salvation*), and **if** they could be renewed again unto repentance *hypothetically*), it would put the Son of God to an open shame.

This text is a favorite among those who are anxious to prove that the saved can be lost and saved again. Our Arminian brethren, who believe that the saved can become lost again, also believe that they can be saved again. But **if** (*hypothetically*) we suppose that this text is teaching that a saved person can become lost again, the verse also says that it would be **impossible** to renew them again unto repentance *(salvation)*. Hence, if (*hypothetically*) a saved person could become lost again it would be impossible for him to be saved again. Consequently, the man-made dogma (*Arminianism)* of a saved person becoming lost and then renewed to salvation is proven to be contradictory. A "so called" second salvation is impossible and is easily disproved by the same text used here in Hebrews chapter 6. Notice that the text is prefaced in a hypothetical sense, **not** in an actual real life situation. Observe the, **For it is impossible** (*Hebrews 6:4*) and the, **if** (*Hebrews 6:6*). The text is saying that it is **impossible** for those who, **if** they were made partakers of the Holy Ghost and known the things of God, to fall away and be renewed again unto repentance. The writer of Hebrews is not saying that a person can fall from salvation; paraphrasing, he is saying, **if they could fall away**, they could not be renewed again unto repentance, thereby crucifying again the Son of God afresh, and putting Him to open shame.

In addressing the **saved** Jews of Hebrews 6:9, the writer of Hebrews said that he is persuaded better things of them than that of the **unbelieving**, legalistic Jews of Hebrews 6:6. He says, But beloved, we are persuaded better things of you, and things that accompany salvation**...**, which things were not of the legalistic Jews mentioned in Hebrews 6:6. The unbelieving Jewish position in Hebrews 6:8 is described as, But that which beareth thorns and briers is rejected and is nigh unto cursing; whose end is to be burned. This is further warning to professors of salvation who are not born again.

◆ *2 Peter 2:20-22: For if after they* (unsaved religionists) *have escaped the pollution of the world through **the knowledge** of the Lord and Saviour Jesus Christ, they are again entangled therein, and overcome, the latter end is worse with them than the beginning. For it had been better for them not to have known **the way** of righteousness, than, after they have known it, to turn from the holy commandment delivered unto them. But it is happened unto them according to the true proverb, The **dog** is turned to his own vomit again; and the **sow** (swine; hog; pig) that was washed to her wallowing in the mire.*

This is another favorite passage that our Arminian brethren use to "allegedly" prove that a saved person can become unsaved. This text is a warning to believers to avoid false teachers. It is also a warning to unsaved Jews who had escaped the pollution of the world through the **knowledge** of Jesus. If the unsaved Jews departed from the way of righteousness, they would return to the way of unrighteousness signified by the uncleanness of the dog and sow.

The false teachers *(unbelievers; dogs; sows)* are plainly identified in preceding verses of chapter 2:

In verse 15, they have **forsaken the right way...**following the way of Balaam...who loved the wages of unrighteousness

In verse 17, these are **called wells without water...**to whom the mist of darkness is reserved for ever

In verse 18, they speak great swelling words of vanity...**they allure through the lusts of the flesh**

In verse 19, while they promise them liberty, they themselves are **the servants of corruption**

In verse 1, they appear as **false teachers who bring in destructive heresies.**

These descriptive terms lead up to the **dog** and **sow** of our text. A genuine believer is never referred to by these terms. A **dog** is alluded to as an unclean, unbelieving Gentile; A **sow** is considered to be an unclean animal. This text is in reference to unsaved teachers and religious professors among the camps of genuine believers. They are likened unto unclean dogs and sows *(not washed from their sins)* who avoided much of the world's pollution by associating with godly people. They would receive a greater condemnation having known the way of righteousness but not having received It. Although these unbelievers had escaped the pollution of the world through the knowledge *(not salvation)* of the Lord, it is quite obvious that they had not been partakers of the divine nature *(2 Peter 1:4)*. They were not changed from a sow or dog into a sheep. The sow was still a sow and the dog was still a dog. God never calls His children either dogs or swine anywhere in the Bible. Sows and dogs symbolize the unclean and those outside the kingdom of God:

Matthew 7:6: Give not that which is holy unto the **dogs** *(unclean Gentiles), neither cast ye your pearls before* **swine** *(unclean mocking sinners) lest they trample them under their feet, and turn again and rend you.*

Jesus Himself also referred to Gentiles as dogs (*Matthew 15:26*). At the time of Christ upon earth, Jews were still under Mosaic Law (the writer believes that the law ceased and NT grace entered when the vail in the Temple was torn – 2 Corinthians 3:14).Gentiles had not yet been corporately (or universally) grafted into the true vine, which is Jesus (*Romans 11:17;John 15:5*).

These false professors (*apostates*) of 2 Peter knew of the way of righteousness but the righteousness of Christ had not been imputed to them. This Scripture is not talking about saved people who became lost and then returned to their vomit and wallowing in the mire; **these are enlightened but unsaved religious people who return to their sin**. These religious pretenders (*dogs and sows)* had not accepted Christ as their Lord and Saviour.

Much pollution of this world is escaped by living in a Christian family or being among godly institutions. Even an **unbelieving husband** is sanctified by his believing wife and the **unbelieving wife** is sanctified by the believing husband (*I Corinthians 7:14*), but that does not mean that these set apart unbelieving spouses are saved.

◆ *Revelation 22:19: And if any man shall take away from the words of the book of this prophecy, God shall take away* **his part** *out of the* **book of life***, and out of the holy city, and from the things which are written in this book.*

In the first place, a genuine Christian will not intentionally take away from the words of God's book of prophecy. The Word of God is the very means whereby a believer has been saved and also his instruction book for life. The acrostic, B-I-B-L-E could be rendered, **B**ible **I**nstructions **B**efore **L**eaving **E**arth.

> *Romans 10:17: So then **faith** cometh by hearing, and hearing by **the Word of God.***

> *I Peter 1:23: Being born again, not of corruptible seed, but of incorruptible, **by the word of God**, which liveth and abideth for ever.*

There is no neutral ground concerning **the Word of God**. You either believe **it all** or you do not believe it **at all** (*you cannot cherry pick*). A truly born-again Christian has great reverence and holy awe for God's "preserved" Word (*We do not have the inspired original autographs, but we do have reliable and true apographs*). Any "so-called" religious person that would intentionally take away from God's Word is not of God; he is playing church (*hypocrite; stage actor; pretender of true religion*).

Whatever Revelation 22:19 is saying, it does not say that God will take away the man's **salvation** or the man's **name** out of the book of life. It does say that God will take **his part** out of the **book of life**. There is a difference between a man's name from a man's part (*allocation*). If this is a time when a saved person is to lose his salvation, the verse would say, God shall take **him** or his **name** out of the book of life, and that would have settled it. What is man's part in the book of life? It is his potential "interest" in salvation and the great privilege of having his name entered into the Book of Life (*The word, part, is also used in John 13:8 and Acts 8:21*). The writer believes that the *provision* of salvation has been made for everyone, **whosoever will** (*Matthew 22:9; John 1:9, 29; 3:16; 6:51; 10:9; 12:32; Acts 10:43; 17:30; Romans 10:13; 11:32; 2 Corinthians 5:14-15; I Timothy 2:4-6; 4:10; Hebrews 2:9; 2 Peter 3:9; I John 2:2; 4:14*).

137

Salvation has been bought and paid for by the shed blood of Jesus Christ for **all men** everywhere, without respect. However, if an *unsaved* person rejects, denies, adds to, deletes, or takes away from the Words of this book of life (*maliciously tampering with God's Word*), God will take away **his part or interest** (*allocation; provision*) out of the book of life. A saved person's **name** would definitely be in the Lamb's book of life but a lost man could only have a part, place, provision, or allocation for his name. The writer believes that the taking away of a part (*allocation for the person's name*) of the Word of God is tantamount to an unpardonable sin and revokes the privilege of a person's name being entered into the Lamb's book of life. However, there are faithful Christians who are of the opinion that all people are listed in the book of life and those that die unsaved will have their names blotted out of this book; the writer offers no argument against this interpretation. God knew those who would be saved before the foundation of the world.

At the White Throne Judgment, the dead (unbelievers) will be judged out of those things which were written in the "books" (not the "book of life"), according to their works (Revelation 22:12, 15)

> **Exodus 32:31-33:** *And Moses returned unto the LORD, and said, Oh, this people have sinned a great sin, and have made them gods of gold. Yet now, if Thou wilt forgive their sin--; and if not, blot me, I pray Thee, out of* **Thy book which Thou hast written**. *And the Lord said unto Moses, Whosoever hath sinned against Me,* **him will I blot out of My book**.

In the first place, there is no reason to believe that this is the book of life of Revelation 3:5. This text of Exodus chapter 32 does not specifically state, "book of life" or "Lamb's book of life," which has never even been mentioned up to this point. This book in Exodus has to do

138

with **Israel under the Covenant of Law and their entry into Canaan**. Moses meant that he would be willing to be excluded from the covenant of God's blessings into Canaan-land in exchange for Israel's sins to be forgiven and their entrance allowed. Salvation is not the subject in this text. This is not a question of Heaven (Paradise)or Hell, but it is **a question of life and death and entering into Canaan blessings**.

Genealogies (*numbering of family pedigree - Numbers 1:18; I Chronicles*) were all peculiar and important to Israel. Records or registers of the tribes were kept so that all of the families could be accounted for (especially the priestly tribe of Levites). The Lord commanded Moses to number Israel (*Numbers 1:19*). Their number determined the distribution of the land of Canaan to the tribes of Israel. A little later, we find that none of those who murmured and were 20 years and older (*Numbers 14:28*) were allowed to enter Canaan. **All of these were blotted out of God's Covenant Book of Promise for Israel's entrance into in Canaan-land.** God is greatly displeased with murmurings. However, Israel's children inherited the land. **Moses,** the lawgiver, was blotted out of Canaan land privileges because of his sin (*Numbers 20:12, 24; 27:13-14; Deuteronomy 3:25-26; 32:51, 52; Psalms 106:33*). Moses was **not** blotted out of The Lamb's Book of Life (*Hebrews 11:23-29*). **Aaron**, the brother of Moses (*directly chosen of God Himself to be the first High Priest*) was also blotted out from entering into Canaan (*Numbers 20:12, 24, 28*). Again, though Moses and Aaron were blotted out of Canaan-land blessing, they were not blotted out of The Lamb's Book of Life.

Israel's evil surmising and rebellion in the wilderness (*Deuteronomy 9:7*) was exceeded by the molten calf image (*Deuteronomy 9:12*). Yet, all Israel was **not** blotted out of entering Canaan-land blessings.

139

◆ *Revelation 3:5:* *He that overcometh, the same shall be clothed in white raiment; and I will not blot out* **his** **name** *out of* **the book of life***, but I will confess* **his** **name** *before My Father, and before His angels.*

This is in reference to saved people in the **Book of Life (***which appears to be the same as the* **Lamb's book of life***)*. It is expressly stated that his **name** (*not, "his part"*) will not be blotted out of the book of life. This Scripture is given to comfort those who endure great tribulation and specifically for those who overcome by the Blood of the Lamb and by the word of their testimony during the Tribulation Period (*Revelation 12:11*). To their great comfort, God promises that **He will not blot out their name out of The Book of Life**. Because this verse says that **God will not blot out their name**, some say that this implies that God will blot out other names. In this verse, there is no doubt as to which book is spoken about; it clearly states that it is The Book of Life. The promise here should clear up any questions concerning those blotted out of The Book of The Covenant of Law in Exodus 32:31-33**. If** the Book of The Covenant of Law (*the book of Exodus 32:31-33)* had been the same as The Book of Life, we would have a clear contradiction of Scriptures.

But, someone may add, Revelation 12:11 says that you have to **overcome**. That is easily settled in Scriptures. We do not overcome the world or the flesh by our own merits or works (*Ephesians 2:8, 9; Titus 3:5)*.

I John 4:4: Ye are of God, little children, and have **overcome** *them:* **because greater is He that is in** **you** *than he that is in the world*

I John 5:4: For **whatsoever is born of God** **overcometh** *the world; and this the victory that overcometh the world, even our faith.*

*I John 5:5: Who is he that **overcometh** the world, but **he that believeth that Jesus is the Son of God.***

*John 6:28-29: Then said they unto Him, What shall we do that we might **work** the works of God?**Jesus answered** and said unto them, **This is the work of God, that ye believe on Him (God the Son; Jesus) whom He hath sent.***

*Revelation 12:11: And they **overcame him by the blood of the Lamb**, and by the word of their testimony; and they loved not their lives unto the death.*

*Philippians 2:13: For it is God which **worketh** in you both to will and to do of His good pleasure.*

◆ ***Ezekiel 3:20-21:*** *Again, When a righteous man doth turn from his righteousness, and commit iniquity, and I lay a stumblingblock before him, he shall die: because thou has not given him warning, he shall die in his sin, and his righteousness which he hath done shall not be remembered: but his blood will I require at thine hand. Nevertheless if thou warn the righteous man, that the righteous sin not, and he doth not sin, he shall surely live, because he is warned; also thou hast delivered thy soul.*

Also refer to Ezekiel 18:24: 33:12-13.

This text has **no** reference to the salvation of a righteous man nor the loss of his soul. The righteousness of the man spoken of is **not** the imputed righteousness of Christ. **It is that man's own righteousness as a citizen under Mosaic Law**. The penalty mentioned here is **not** the eternal damnation of Hell but of **physical death**. If a righteous Jew, who had committed no sin or crime before, should turn from his righteous ways and commit iniquity, he should be punished just as any other guilty law-breaker. The offending Jew's past record of righteous living offered no protection from punishment under covenant law. This is parallel to our jurisprudence system of law. If an upstanding citizen commits murder, his good citizenship and moral life does not protect him from the guilt and deserved punishment of the offense. Good citizenship of all is expected. Having committed an offense for the "first time" does not void the punishment of the crime.

If this righteous man should be in reference to a genuine believer, it would appear to be an admonition of the responsible person to warn the righteousness man of an untimely death (*sin unto death*). If the righteous man heeded the warning, he would live and the person who warned him would not have blood on his hand.

The only salvation mentioned in the context (*Ezekiel 3:18),* is a warning to the righteous man to not sin and save his **physical life**

◆ ***Colossians 1:21-23:*** *And you, that were sometime alienated (before salvation) and enemies in your mind by wicked works,* ***yet now hath He reconciled****. In the body of His flesh through death, to present you holy and unblameable and unreproveable in His sight:* ***If*** *ye continue in the faith grounded and settled, and be not moved away from the hope of the gospel, which ye have heard, and which was preached to every creature which is under heaven; whereof I Paul am made a minister.*

In this text, the "if" is not questioning the fact of their salvation but assumes that they are saved. Paul, in effect, said, If ye died with Christ, and if ye were raised with Christ. Now the writer does not believe that it is essential to know Greek or Hebrew to arrive at a correct interpretation of Scripture. A Christian brother's comments on this text of Colossians are helpful. **C. F. Baker** says that there are five classes of conditional sentences in the Greek. When **if** (ei) is followed by the

"Indicative" mood as it is in the above scripture and also in chapters 2:20 and 3:1, the hypothesis is assumed as an actual fact, the condition being unfilled, but no doubt being thrown on the supposition. Notice all the "ifs" in verses 12-19. All seven of these "ifs" are used in the same construction as in Colossians 1:23. When **if** (ean) is followed by the "Subjunctive" mood, as it is in Colossians 3:13 and 4:10, it expresses a hypothetical but possible condition, contingent on circumstances which the future will reveal. **Their continuing in faith was the evidence that they had been reconciled.**

When Paul said, "**If** the dead rise not," he was surely not casting doubt on the facts of the resurrection."

Emphasis of Eternal Life

Everyone will exist forever regardless of their spiritual condition (*saved and lost*). Upon death, all believers go to Heaven forever and all unsaved sinners will ultimately be consigned to the lake of fire forever (this is the second death of the lost - *Revelation 20:13-15*).

The false dogma of soul-annihilation (*taught by several false religions*) is not found in the Scriptures. If the **sinner** does not come to Christ for eternal life, they will exist forever, suffering everlasting destruction from the presence of the Lord (*I Thessalonians 1:9*). The lake of fire is the final abode where the worm dieth not and the fire is not quenched (*Mark 9:42-47*). Vain philosophies of secular sources do not matter.

If one has not yet trusted in Christ for Everlasting Life, the only life remaining is one of uncertainty, doubt, fear, and torment (*Death is the king of terror for the lost man*).Of course, the joy of eternal life is a present possession requiring faith in God's promise for those who are presumptuous enough to receive it.

143

*I Corinthians 1:20, 22: For **all the promises of God** in Him are **yea**, and in Him **amen**, unto the glory of God by us. **Who** hath also **sealed us** and given the earnest of the Spirit in our hearts.*

Doctrine of Eternal Life

Our Arminian brethren reason that the doctrine of eternal life (*eternal security*) leads one to a life of careless living (*antinomianism*). They say that a person who believes that he is guaranteed of going to Heaven will continue to live comfortably in his sin. The writer believes that this may be true for **unsaved professors** and those that lightly regard scriptural teachings, but not so for brethren who believe in eternal life.

Arminian brethren also erroneously believe that a careful life of good works, self-discipline, and one of his own steadfastness in the faith, will guarantee his continuance of salvation. An Arminian brother actually told this writer that he was guaranteed of Heaven because of his life of sinless perfection. While this is untrue, it is to the credit of our Arminian brethren to insist upon a holy life for Christians. Many that name the name of Christ do not even attempt to live a holy life (*as some apostate Baptists*). No matter how much a Christian tries, he cannot live in an absolute perfect fashion as to guarantee the continual duration of his salvation. The Holy Spirit is our guarantor of eternal life (*Ephesians 1:13; 4:30; 2 Corinthians 1:20-22*). The Holy Spirit abides within the believer forever (*John 14:16; Romans 8:9*).

The writer has observed that some Arminian brethren return to a sinful life because they believed that they had lost their salvation due to a carnal fault or careless slip. These brethren (seemingly oblivious of their abiding carnal nature) reckoned that they were no longer saved, so they relaxed their moral standards and gradually fell into sin. Of course, Arminian brethren believe that they can lose their salvation and hopeful that they can be saved again. A mature Christian, who is rooted and grounded in God's Word, **knows** that the carnal nature of man has not been done away with (*Romans chapter 7),* and he does not easily return to a life of sin.

A mature Christian knowledgeable in God's Word, knows that he is privileged to confess and forsake his sin (*I John 1:8-9; 2:1-2*), and to continue on in his Christian sojourn. Spiritually minded Christians know that the believer has two natures that war against each other, the flesh nature and the new spiritual man in Christ. It appears that many of our Arminian brethren have not yet fully realized the constant warfare between the two abiding natures of the believer. During the entire fifty years this writer has been saved, he has never heard an Arminian brother preach or teach on the subject of two opposing natures (*2 Peter 1:4; I Corinthians 3:2-4; Hebrews 5:12*). I am confident that some have.

<u>The believer does not keep himself saved</u>:

Galatians 3:3: Are ye so foolish? having begun in the Spirit, are ye now made perfect by the flesh?

Anyone depending upon keeping the law to remain saved would have to keep the whole law and not offend in one point if he or she ever expected to get to Heaven.

James 2:10: **For whosoever shall keep the whole law, and yet offend in one point, he is guilty of all.**

<u>Law Keeping and Works Cannot Be Mingled or Mixed With Grace</u>

Romans 11:6: And if by grace, then is it **no more of works***: otherwise grace is no more grace. But if it be of works, then is it no more grace: otherwise work is no more work.*

Salvation is From Faith to Faith

Romans 1:17: For therein is the righteousness of God revealed **from faith to faith**: as it is written, The just shall live by faith (See *also Romans 1:13; 3:27; 14:23*).

It is not, from faith to works, as if faith put us into a justified state, and then works preserved and maintained us in it; but it is, from faith to faith. We are changed into the same image of the glory of the Lord by the Spirit of the Lord (*2 Corinthians 3:18*).

> *Galatians 3:1-3: O FOOLISH Galatians, **who hath bewitched you**, that ye should not obey the truth, before whose eyes Jesus Christ hath been evidently set forth, crucified among you? This only would I learn of you, **Received ye the Spirit by the works of the law, or by the hearing of faith? Are ye so foolish? Having begun in the Spirit, are ye now made perfect by the flesh?***

The Just are: Saved by **faith** (Ephesians 2:8); Live by **faith** (Habakkuk 2:4; Romans *1:17*); Walk by **faith** (*Romans 4:12; 2 Corinthians 5:7*); K**ept** through **faith** by the power of God (*I Peter1:5*). Salvation is, all of grace, both the saving and the keeping (*Ephesians 2:8; Romans 11:6; I Peter 1:5*)

> *Ephesians 2:8-9: For **by grace** are ye saved through faith; and that not of yourselves: it is the gift of God: Not of works, lest any man should boast.*

> *Romans 6:14: For sin shall not have dominion over you: for ye are not under the law, but under **grace.***

> *Romans 11:6: And if by grace, then is it no more of works: otherwise grace is no more grace. But if it be of works, then is it no more grace: otherwise work is no more work.*

*Romans 10:9-10, 13: That if thou shalt confess with thy mouth the Lord Jesus, and shalt believe in thine heart that God hath raised Him from the dead, thou shalt be saved. For with the heart man believeth unto righteousness; and with the mouth confession is made unto salvation. For **whosoever** shall call upon the name of the Lord shall be saved.*

The Christian is **Sealed** with the Holy Spirit of Promise **Unto** the Resurrection

*Ephesians 4:30: And grieve not the Holy Spirit of God, whereby ye are **sealed unto the day of redemption.***

(**Note:** Grammatically speaking, the word, until, might possibly suggest a momentary break in time, whereas the word, unto, allows no chronological break in time at all.)

*Ephesians 1:13: In whom ye also trusted, after that ye heard the word of truth, the gospel of your salvation; in whom also after that ye believed, ye were **sealed with that Holy Spirit** of promise.*

*2 Corinthians 1:22: Who hath s**ealed us**, and **given the earnest of the Spirit** in our hearts.*

*John 6:27: Labour not for the meat which perisheth, but for that meat which endureth unto everlasting life, which the Son of man shall give unto you: **for him** (the believer) **hath God the Father sealed.***

Believers are Preserved (not pickled as some Arminian brethren jest in ridicule):

- *Psalms 37:28: For the LORD loveth judgment, and forsaketh not His saints: they are **preserved for ever**: but the seed of the wicked shall be cut off.*

- *Psalms 97:10: Ye that love the LORD, hate evil: **He preserveth the souls of His saints**; He delivereth them out of the hand of the wicked.*

147

- *Psalms 121:3, 5, 7: He will not suffer thy foot to be moved: He that **keepeth thee** will not slumber. The LORD is **Thy keeper**: The LORD shall **preserve thee** from all evil: He shall **preserve thy soul**.*

- *2 Timothy 4:18: And the Lord shall **deliver me** from every evil work, and will **preserve me unto His heavenly kingdom**: to whom be glory for ever and ever .Amen.*

- *Jude 1:1:Jude, the servant of Jesus Christ, and brother of James, to them that are sanctified by God the Father, and **preserved in Jesus Christ**, and called.*

If (*hypothetically*) this writer believed that he could become lost again, his constant petition to God, night and day, would be for God to take his life while he remained saved.

If (*hypothetically*) a saved person could become lost again, **why** would an omniscient, all-loving, all powerful, compassionate God wait until a saved person was unsaved (*hypothetically, of course*) to allow him to die. The Compassionate Father would surely take his life before he "allegedly" became unsaved. God is omniscient and knows all things before time.

If this writer had honest doubts concerning abiding eternal life (permanence *of salvation*), he would seek to mourn in sackcloth and ashes (*Esther 4:1, 3; Isaiah 37:1; 58:5; Daniel 9:3*).

Eternal Life brethren are convinced that ALL of their sins are forgiven and will be remembered against them no more (*Hebrews 8:12*). They are convinced of having **everlasting life** imputed to them and never again will be condemned to Hell (*John 3:18; 5:24; 17:12; Romans 8:1; Philippians 1:28; Hebrews 10:39; Romans 8:29-30*).

Disclaimer

The writer disclaims any intention of casting doubts upon the integrity of my Arminian and Hyper-Calvinist brethren; the writer loves both, regardless of our differences in doctrinal positions. This writer does not consider any one of the three groups to be spiritually superior to the other two. One day, God will correct all of us. We (*all saved people)* are in the same family of the kingdom of God).

A Greater Blessing of Salvation

Salvation is a far greater blessing when one fully realizes that he is presently **saved foreve**r and has, right now, eternal life, and will not become lost again *(Romans 8:1; I John 3:2, 3*). It is far better to be saved and **know** it (*I John 5:13)* and have the **full assurance** (*Hebrews 6:11; 10:22)* of its **continual performance** (*Philippians 1:6; Ecclesiastes 3:14; John 10:27-29),* than to be saved without full assurance.

> *2 Timothy 1:12: For the which cause I also suffer these things: nevertheless I am not ashamed:* **for I know** *Whom I have believed, and am* **persuaded that He is able to keep** *that which I have committed unto Him against that day.*

Paul knew for sure that he had committed his **soul** to the Lord, and that God was able to **keep** it against that future day.

> *Romans 8:38-39: For* **I am persuaded***, that neither death, nor life, nor angels, nor principalities, nor powers, nor things present, nor things to come, Nor height, nor depth, nor any other creature, shall be able to separate us from the love of God, which is in Christ Jesus our Lord.*

If we ourselves could or would remove ourselves from God's salvation, this would have been a most excellent time for the Spirit of God to have plainly told us. Paul was **persuaded** otherwise. Can the reader think of anything not included in this text?

<u>There may be times when the child of God is cast down, but he is never cast off</u>

> *Psalms 94:14: For the LORD will not cast off His people, neither will He forsake his inheritance.*

> *I Peter 1:4-5: To an inheritance incorruptible, and undefiled, and that fadeth not away, reserved in heaven for you, Who are kept by the power of God through faith unto salvation ready to be revealed in the last time*

> *Hebrews 13:5: Let your conversation be without covetousness; and be content with such things as ye have: for He hath said, I will never leave thee, nor forsake thee.*

Conclusion of Eternal Security

No one will convince another by debating over isolated passages of Scripture that may be impertinent or misapplied to the subject of salvation. Salvation is a gift of the grace of God and received through faith alone. A man can do nothing either to save himself or to keep himself saved; if he could, then salvation would be at least, in part by works, which the Word of God emphatically refutes. We are not saved because we are good and we are not lost because we are bad. A child of God may be a disobedient child, but he remains a child of God, and for his disobedience he must reckon with a faithful Father who will deal with him as with a son and not as a bastard (*Hebrews 12:8*).

Jesus Smitten Only Once and No More

> *Hebrews 9:28: So Christ was once offered to bear the sins of many…*

150

> *Hebrews 9:26: "...But* **now once in the end of the world** *hath He (Jesus) appeared to put away sin by the sacrifice of Himself.*

Christ came ONLY ONCE to die for sinners. There will never be another Calvary. **Eternal Life** is determined by whether or not a person has the Son of God abiding within. He that hath the Son hath Eternal Life and he that believeth not the Son of God shall not see life (*I John 5:11; 3:23; 2:27; 2 John 9; Romans 8:9-11; John 3:18, 36*).

Believers trusting in Jesus Christ are **saved**, **indwelt**, **taught**, **sanctified**, and **sealed** with the Holy Spirit of promise (I Corinthians 12:13; Titus 3:5; Romans 8:9; John 16:7, 13; Romans 15:16; I Corinthians 6:11; Jude 1; Ephesians 1:13; 4:30; 2 Corinthians 1:22).

> *Romans 8:16: The Spirit Itself beareth witness with our spirit, that we are the children of God.*

> *Psalms 34:19: Many are the afflictions of the righteous:* **but the LORD delivereth him out of them all.**

God speaks to the unsaved man:

God does not force Himself upon anyone. It is the work of the small, still voice of the Holy Spirit to convince and convict a sinner of his lost condition and his need of the Saviour. The sinner will either **believe** the Gospel and receive eternal life (*John 3:16*), or **disbelieve (***or neglect***)**, and be eternally lost (*John 3:18, 36; Hebrews 2:3*).

> *John 5:40: And* **ye will not** *come to Me, that ye might have life.*

> *Hebrews 9:27: And as it is appointed unto man once to die but after this the judgment.*

*Romans 6:23: For the wages of sin is death, but the **gift of God is eternal life** through Jesus Christ our Lord.*

*John 6:39-40: And this is the Father's will which hath sent Me, that of all which He hath given Me **I should lose nothing**, but should raise it up again at the last day. And this is the will of Him that sent Me, that **every one** which seeth the Son, and **believeth on Him**, may have **everlasting life**: and I will raise him up at the last day.*

*Ephesians 2:8-9: For by grace are ye saved through faith; and that not of yourselves; it is the **gift** of God: Not of works, lest any man should boast.*

Romans 10:9-10: That if thou shalt confess with thy mouth the Lord Jesus, and shalt believe in thine heart that God hath raised Him (Jesus) from the dead, thou shalt be saved. For with the heart man believeth unto righteousness: and with the mouth confession is made unto salvation.

*Romans 10:13: For **whosoever** shall call upon the name of the Lord shall be saved.*

Galatians 6:3: For if a man think himself to be something, when he is nothing, he deceiveth himself.

Dennis Helton
200 Home Place Drive
Easley, SC 29640

ABOUT THE AUTHOR

The writer was born in Greenville, SC in 1934 and was a lifetime resident with the exception of two years in the US Army (Fort Jackson, S.C. and Fort Carson, Colorado) and two years residence in Florida.

After separation (honorably) from the US Army, the writer returned to Greenville, SC and married at age 27 to Christine Moore, an old acquaintance from an adjacent neighborhood. The Lord blessed us with six daughters, Debbie, Donna, Dale, Denise, Deree, and Dena. The Heltons are also presently blessed with eleven grandchildren and three great-grandchildren.

A short time after marriage, the writer was convicted of his lost condition as a sinner and after a miserable time under conviction the writer confessed his sin and lost condition to God and was saved.

The writer was 40 years of age when he began attending college (3 years, no diploma).

The writer retired as a chemical technologist from Morton International Chemical Company in 1996. Before retirement, the writer had the urge to write on Bible subjects and wished that he had more time to study. Upon retirement, the writer bought a computer and became a novice writer.

D. Helton has written several books and booklets documents such as, "Jesus is God," "Evolution, Another False Religion of Humanism," "Cremation: Christian or Pagan?", "Is The Gap Theory Credible?" and others which are available here and in many online bookstores such as

Amazon, Thrift Books, Books-A-Million, Barnes & Noble, and
http://www.theoldpathspublications.com/Pages/Authors/Helton.htm#God

The writer enjoys Bible study, and especially Bible prophecy, which is future history written in advance. The Bible is history past, history present, and history future (Revelation 1:19).

www.ingramcontent.com/pod-product-compliance
Lightning Source LLC
Chambersburg PA
CBHW051841090426
42736CB00011B/1913